Incorporating Foreign Language Content in Humanities Courses

Incorporating Foreign Language Content in Humanities Courses introduces innovative ways to integrate aspects of foreign language study into courses containing humanities concepts.

The edited collection offers case studies from various universities and across multiple languages. It serves as a useful guide to all foreign language faculty with any language expertise (as well as others interested in promoting foreign languages) for the adaptation and development of their own curricula. Infusing foreign language content into English-taught humanities courses helps promote languages as practical and relevant to students.

It will be of interest to language educators, including teachers, teachers-in-training, teacher educators, and administrators.

Priya Ananth is an Associate Professor of Japanese in the Department of World Languages, Literatures, and Cultures at Middle Tennessee State University.

Leah Tolbert Lyons is an Associate Professor of French in the Department of World Languages, Literatures, and Cultures at Middle Tennessee State University.

Incorporating Foreign Language Content in Humanities Courses

Edited by Priya Ananth and Leah Tolbert Lyons

LONDON AND NEW YORK

First published 2020
by Routledge
2 Park Square, Milton Park, Abingdon, Oxon OX14 4RN
and by Routledge
605 Third Avenue, New York, NY 10017

First issued in paperback 2021

Routledge is an imprint of the Taylor & Francis Group, an informa business

© 2020 selection and editorial matter, Priya Ananth and Leah Tolbert Lyons; individual chapters, the contributors

The right of Priya Ananth and Leah Tolbert Lyons to be identified as the authors of the editorial material, and of the authors for their individual chapters, has been asserted in accordance with sections 77 and 78 of the Copyright, Designs and Patents Act 1988.

All rights reserved. No part of this book may be reprinted or reproduced or utilised in any form or by any electronic, mechanical, or other means, now known or hereafter invented, including photocopying and recording, or in any information storage or retrieval system, without permission in writing from the publishers.

Trademark notice: Product or corporate names may be trademarks or registered trademarks, and are used only for identification and explanation without intent to infringe.

British Library Cataloguing-in-Publication Data
A catalogue record for this book is available from the British Library

Library of Congress Cataloging-in-Publication Data
A catalog record has been requested for this book

ISBN 13: 978-0-367-78785-1 (pbk)
ISBN 13: 978-0-367-34348-4 (hbk)

Typeset in Times New Roman
by codeMantra

Contents

List of figures	viii
List of tables	ix
List of contributors	x
Acknowledgments	xiii

Introduction	1

PART I
Literature
13

1 Linking language and literature 15
   LEAH TOLBERT LYONS

2 A bilingual approach to a humanities course: enriching Japanese learning through translating flash fiction into English 25
   CATHERINE RYU

3 Engaging language policies and poetics in an African literature classroom 34
   JULIE HUNTINGTON

4 Finding meaning in translation: critical reading for Japanese literature and film in translation 43
   CHIAKI TAKAGI

5 Spanish Golden Age literature in the general education curriculum: sharing the riches of culture and language 52
CHARLENE KALINOSKI

PART II 61
Linguistics

6 Japanese and English in contact: linguistic and cultural perspectives 63
PRIYA ANANTH

7 Understanding key sociocultural concepts in Japanese: unlocking the door to communication 77
KATHY NEGRELLI

8 Approaching language issues critically: language in Japanese society 87
RIKA ITO

9 Japanese sociolinguistics: Reacting to the Past and beyond 96
NORIKO AKIMOTO SUGIMORI

10 Language, identity, and power in Japan: gender in Japanese language 104
JUNKO UENO

PART III 113
Culture

11 Teaching *katakana* in a cool Japan culture course 115
YUMIKO TASHIRO

12 Understanding Chinese behavioral culture through cross-cultural communication 124
JUNQING (JESSIE) JIA

13 Introducing the Portuguese language through Brazilian popular culture 133
SORAYA CALHEIROS NOGUEIRA

Contents vii

14 Culture and language appreciation in a history of Latin America course   141
BEATRIZ GARCÍA GLICK

15 Heroes and Heroínas: teaching myths and legends through Hispanic culture   149
TIFFANY GAGLIARDI TROTMAN

Conclusion   161

Index   165

Figures

I.1	Fall Language Enrollments by Year (1958–2016)	2
6.1	My Switch 1	67
6.2	My Switch 2	68
6.3	Resortful	69
6.4	Eki na Cafe	70
6.5	Sunao	71
6.6	Tomodachi Burger	72
11.1	Emoji Created by Student	120
11.2	Sample Pages from a Student *Manga* Project	121

Tables

7.1	Sample Lesson Plan	82
12.1	Final Project Rubric	130
15.1	Assessment Chart for SPAN 250 Course (Intermediate)	151
15.2	Assessment Chart for SPAN 350 Course (Advanced)	152
15.3	Thematic Units	153
15.4	Weekly Class Activities	154

Contributors

Priya Ananth is an Associate Professor of Japanese in the Department of World Languages, Literatures, and Cultures at Middle Tennessee State University. She earned her Ph.D. in East Asian Languages and Literatures from The Ohio State University. Her teaching and research focus on issues related to applied Japanese linguistics, Japanese second language acquisition, and Japanese pedagogy.

Beatriz García Glick earned a Doctorate in Modern Languages from Middlebury College, in Middlebury, Vermont. She is an Associate Teaching Professor of Spanish and French in the Humanities Department at the Pennsylvania State University, Hazleton campus, in Pennsylvania.

Julie Huntington is an Associate Professor of English and World Literatures at Marymount Manhattan College. She earned her Ph.D. in French from Vanderbilt University. She is the author of *Sounding Off: Rhythm, Music, and Identity in West African and Caribbean Francophone Novels*.

Rika Ito is an Associate Professor of Japanese in the Asian Studies Department at St. Olaf College. She received her Ph.D. in Linguistics from Michigan State University. Her research interests include analyzing the role of language ideology in popular media, applying research findings to Japanese language instruction, and conducting research with students.

Junqing (Jessie) Jia is an Assistant Professor of Chinese in the Department of East Asian Languages and Literatures at Hamilton College. Jia received her Doctorate in Chinese Language Pedagogy from The Ohio State University in 2017. Jia's research focuses on understanding foreign language learning motivation and creating motivating experiences in the classroom and beyond.

Contributors xi

Charlene Kalinoski, Ph.D., teaches Spanish in the Department of Modern Languages at Roanoke College in Salem, Virginia. Her course offerings span the Spanish curriculum: language, literature, culture, and short-term study abroad. The course described in this volume represents her contribution to the humanities requirement of the college's general education curriculum.

Leah Tolbert Lyons is an Associate Professor of French in the Department of World Languages, Literatures, and Cultures at Middle Tennessee State University. Having earned her Ph.D. from Vanderbilt University, her research and teaching are mutually informed and center on francophone literature and film from Africa and its Diaspora.

Kathy Negrelli, Ph.D., is an Associate Professor of Japanese in the Department of Foreign Languages at Kennesaw State University where she teaches JPN 1001–3000-level skills courses and coordinates the Japanese program. Her research interests include acculturation, intercultural competence, and the use of technology in the foreign language classroom.

Soraya Calheiros Nogueira is an Associate Professor of Spanish and Portuguese in the Department of World Languages, Literatures, and Cultures at Middle Tennessee State University where she teaches Portuguese and Spanish languages, literatures, and cultures. Her area of specialization is 20th-century Latin American Literatures and Cultures.

Catherine Ryu, Ph.D., is an Associate Professor of Japanese Culture and Literature in the Department of Linguistics and Languages at Michigan State University. She specializes in classical Japanese, including Heian narratives and poetry. Her teaching and research interests include digital humanities, Zainichi studies, graphic narratives, and game studies.

Noriko Akimoto Sugimori is an Associate Professor and Chair of the Japanese Program at Kalamazoo College. She received her Ph.D. in Applied Linguistics from Boston University. Her research interests include sociolinguistics, language ideology, and language policy.

Chiaki Takagi is a Senior Lecturer of Japanese and Asian Studies in the Department of Languages, Literatures, and Cultures at the University of North Carolina at Greensboro (UNCG). She earned her Ph.D. in English with a concentration in postcolonial literature from UNCG. Her primary research subject is the contemporary Japanese writer Haruki Murakami.

Yumiko Tashiro is a Visiting Assistant Professor of Japanese in the Department of Modern Languages and Literatures at Kenyon College, where she teaches Japanese language courses. She received her Ph.D. from Purdue University. Her chapter in this volume emerged out of a course she taught at Washington and Lee University in 2016 and 2017.

Tiffany Gagliardi Trotman is an Associate Professor in the Department of Languages and Cultures at the University of Otago, New Zealand. She holds a B.A. in Spanish and Politics from Washington and Lee University, an M.A. from the University of Virginia and a Ph.D. from the University of Otago. Her research includes contemporary Spanish culture, pilgrimage studies, and higher education.

Junko Ueno is an Associate Professor in the Department of Modern Languages and Literatures at Union College, Schenectady, New York. She received her Ph.D. in Language Education from Indiana University, Bloomington, Indiana. Her language specialization is Japanese, and her research interests include foreign language pedagogy, gender linguistics, learner motivation, and bilingualism.

Acknowledgments

We wish to express our gratitude to everyone who became a part of our project. First, we thank the chapter contributors for sharing their course materials and expertise, which made this volume possible. We also thank Dr. Judith Rusciolelli, Dr. Tom Brinthaupt, and Dr. Karen Petersen for their valuable feedback at the initial stages of the project. We are grateful to Dr. Karen Petersen (Dean, College of Liberal Arts, Middle Tennessee State University) and Dr. Roger Pieroni (Chair, Department of World Languages, Literatures, and Cultures, Middle Tennessee State University) for their support and encouragement. We appreciate the assistance of the entire editorial team: Samantha Vale Noya, Rosie McEwan, Nick Craggs (Routledge), Assunta Petrone (codeMantra) and everyone involved with copyediting, typesetting and production for their professionalism. Last but not least, we thank our families for their patience and for believing in us.

Priya Ananth and Leah Tolbert Lyons

Introduction

Declining enrollments in foreign languages and humanities

Most foreign language teachers in America can tell you that enrollment in their college classes has been steadily declining over time. This type of anecdotal observation is confirmed by the Modern Language Association of America (MLA), who has been tracking course enrollments in languages other than English at the undergraduate and graduate levels for the past 60 years. Recent surveys conducted by the MLA point to not-so-encouraging trends in foreign language enrollments across the United States in recent years. According to one MLA report, enrollments in languages other than English fell 9.2% in American colleges and universities in the United States between fall 2013 and fall 2016, and this was the second largest drop on record, with the largest being 12.6% in 1972 (Looney et al.). According to a recent article in *The Chronicle of Higher Education*, citing a forthcoming MLA report, "colleges closed more than 650 foreign language programs in a recent three-year period" (Johnson par. 1). There is a clear correlation between the elimination of language programs and the decrease in foreign language student enrollment (Johnson par. 10).

As we see, declines in enrollments have occurred at various moments over time. In the new millennium, historical events such as the terrorist attacks of 9/11 in the United States and the Great Recession of 2008/2009, which affected many countries simultaneously, changed the landscape of higher education, particularly the humanities and foreign languages. After 9/11, higher education manifested itself as a "dynamic, rapidly changing environment marked by a sense of crisis around what came to be called the nation's language deficit" (Geisler et al. 234). At that particular time, the value of language was readily acknowledged, due to communication gaps in certain critical languages

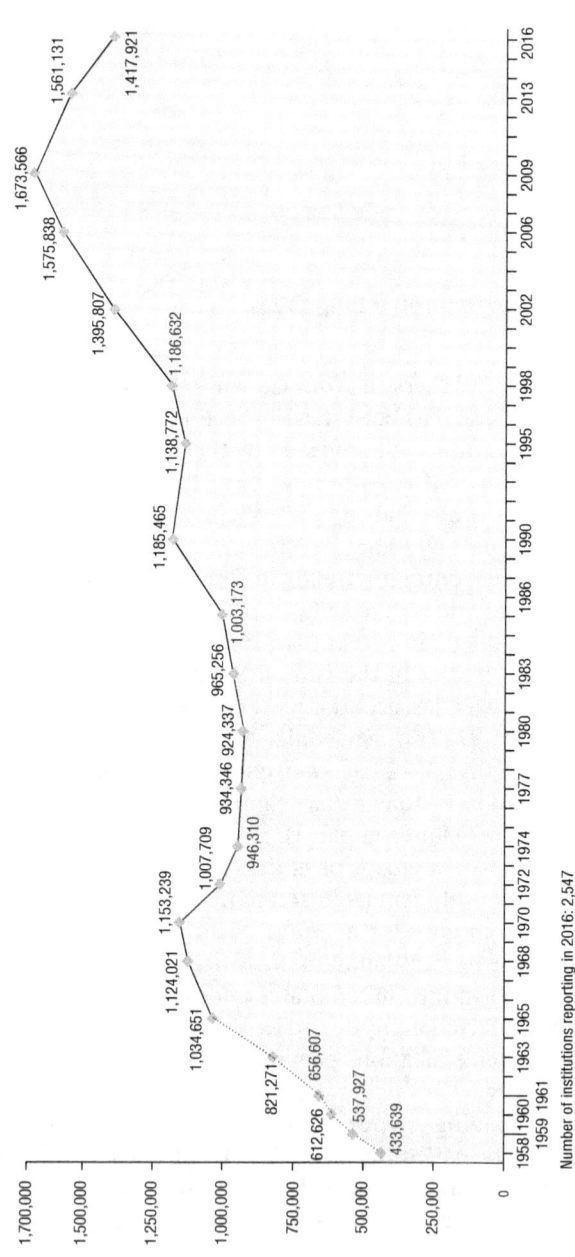

Figure 1.1 Fall Language Enrollments by Year (1958–2016).
Source: Figure from "Enrollments in Languages Other Than English in United States Institutions of Higher Education," *Summer 2016 and Fall 2016: Preliminary Report*. © 2018 Modern Language Association of America.

such as Arabic. While for some, language learning may be seen simply as "a skill to use for communicating thought and information" (Geisler et al. 235), language educators know that "learning a language is more than learning grammar, especially in a transnational world" (Mignolo 1239). Indeed, "Language is a complex multifunctional phenomenon that links an individual to other individuals, to communities, and to national cultures" (Geisler et al. 235), which is at "the core of translingual and transcultural competence" (Geisler et al. 235). While the goals of language learning may be disputed and while these varying opinions may lead to different approaches to foreign language teaching, the post-9/11 worldview saw the value of foreign language study as indisputable (Geisler et al. 235). Yet only a few years after the global financial crisis foreign language enrollments started to fall, as shown in Figure I.1.

Historically speaking, there has been a steep decline in university enrollments in the years following a severe recession in economy, namely in 1972, 1990, and 2009. The recession of 2008/2009 seemed to impact foreign language programs more severely than other programs in the humanities (Johnson par. 15). Indeed after the first recession recorded in 1972, which as we have seen marks the sharpest decline in foreign language enrollments, the need to address this decline became a matter for discussion in the profession. Addressing this issue, language educator Sonja Karsen states,

> Those of us presently engaged in the teaching of foreign languages and literatures on the college or university level cannot help but notice that the ever decreasing enrollment figures in our discipline have affected our attitudes, methods and techniques. Recent statistics prove that the outlook is bleak indeed, unless we can come up with a solution that will reverse the trend reported by the Modern Language Association in its Fall 1974 survey. (Karsen 3)

Although recession was clearly a factor in declining enrollments in foreign language classes in the 1970s, the current decline may be attributed to multiple factors. While some would contend that enrollments in foreign language classrooms may ebb and flow on the basis of social, economic, or political climate, the current trend is compounded by the fact that declining enrollments in foreign language classrooms have occurred against a larger backdrop of decreasing enrollments in the humanities disciplines overall during the past 15 years, according to Humanities Departmental Surveys from 2008 to 2013. Additional causes of decreasing enrollments beyond the economic downturn remain a subject of debate. In light of the diversity of methods used in classrooms, the wide variety of teaching approaches, and the charismatic personalities of foreign language teachers, there could be nothing inherent to the discipline to account for a nationwide decline in enrollments. National trends in education may provide some insight: "Some academics point to colleges' prioritization of STEM programs, or to the long-term effects of colleges' dropping language requirements" (Johnson par. 11). Such changes have precipitated cuts in language programs nationwide. In "Colleges Lose a 'Stunning' 651 Foreign Language Programs in 3 Years," the director of education at the American Council on Teaching Foreign Languages (ACTFL), Paul Sandrock, makes the link between declining enrollments and cuts in foreign language programs (Johnson par. 14). Cutting language programs may be a ready solution to budgetary considerations and decreasing revenues; however, such solutions have been detrimental to foreign language education and consequently to education overall.

Dwindling enrollments in humanities disciplines is alarming because a humanities education, including foreign language study, directly contributes to the development of critical thinking skills and cultural intelligence. In his book, *In Defense of a Liberal Education*, Fareed Zakaria asserts that certain humanities fields

> ...often require the intensive study of several languages and cultures, experience working in foreign countries, an eye for aesthetics, and the ability to translate from one medium or culture to another. Most of these skills could be useful in any number of professions in today's globalized age. They force you to look at people and objects from a variety of perspectives. (87)

The importance of a humanities education, including foreign language programs, is clear. As such, decisions to cut language programs only serve to undermine the development of critical thinking skills and cultural intelligence, which are needful in all career fields, without regard to discipline-specific training. As Zakaria goes on to say regarding a humanities education that prioritizes the study of language and culture, "...this kind of exposure trains various kinds of intelligence, making you a more creative and aware person" (87). Hence, it is clear that we can neither overlook the importance of offering courses in humanities and foreign languages nor ignore the reality of declining enrollments and cuts in foreign language programs. The concepts presented in this volume address this critical need and growing concern. We propose the presentation of foreign language content in courses taught in English to students who may or may not have any previous knowledge of a target language, as a means of attracting students to foreign language study.

Combining foreign languages and humanities content – early approaches

Over time, various attempts have been made to combine foreign languages with content courses taught in English. However, among them are those that emphasize approaches to foreign language teaching. The present volume does not address foreign language pedagogy; rather, it provides a way to introduce foreign language content and concepts to students as a strategy for recruiting them into foreign language classrooms. With this in mind, it is useful to understand past approaches to teaching foreign languages with humanities content. For example, Content-Based Instruction (CBI) finds its basis in cognitive psychology and may be defined as "the integration of particular content with language-teaching aims" and "refers to the concurrent teaching of academic subject matter and second language skills" (Brinton et al. 2). Brinton et al. note in the updated edition of their seminal work *Content-Based Second Language Instruction* that "current research on sociocultural theory and sociopolitical issues in second language learning has also influenced developments in CBI, particularly the recognition that L2 learning takes place within complex social and cultural contexts" (245). Therefore, in CBI, the marriage of language and content provides a context to increase the efficacy of language instruction and, consequently, the proficiency of language students.

Various offshoots of CBI provide for the application and development of foreign language learning through courses in other disciplines that are taught in English. Language educator Emily Spinelli explains that in the field of foreign language education, "curricular innovations that allow students to apply their knowledge of a language other than English in courses outside language departments and/or integrate other disciplines into language courses are designated by two widely known terms – Languages Across the Curriculum (LAC) or Foreign Languages Across the Curriculum (FLAC)" (Spinelli 13). LAC/FLAC is designed to bring other disciplines into foreign language courses to enhance student language learning through the enrichment of content other than what would be taught in language classes.

While there are many variations of LAC/FLAC as curricular approaches to foreign language proficiency, we will examine the two models that are most apropos to this volume. First, there is the export model.

In this paradigm, "a fourth hour of foreign language is added to a normal three-hour section of a humanities or social science course taught in English. In the fourth hour, selected texts that highlight some aspect of the discipline course are presented and discussed in the target language" (Bettencourt 55). In other words, a foreign language component is simply added to a discipline-specific course. Next, there is the import model where "faculty outside of the foreign language department who are proficient in a second language serve as guest lectures in the language class and present some aspect of their discipline" (Bettencourt 55). In this formula, experts from a given discipline come into foreign language classrooms to provide content instruction for language students. As Spinelli makes explicit, the export model refers to "programs that use language materials in courses outside the language department," while the import model refers to "programs that integrate materials from other disciplines into language courses" (Spinelli 13). Both models support the combination of foreign languages and discipline-specific courses with the goal of increasing language proficiency through a content area.

The implementation of approaches such as CBI and LAC/FLAC often requires grant funding to support such initiatives. This was the case at Earlham College, where the CBI approach was implemented through support from the National Endowment for the Humanities (NEH) (Jurasek 52), and St. Olaf College where FLAC was developed through NEH funding as well (Allen et al. 13). What is needed, however, is an alternative for foreign language educators that increases foreign language enrollments without a costly investment of time and money. This book provides that alternative because it presents course samples that, unlike LAC/FLAC, incorporate foreign languages into a course facilitated by a language expert in a single classroom where a humanities content course is being taught. The purpose of this volume is to introduce innovative ways of integrating aspects of foreign languages into courses containing humanities concepts. More specifically, this book represents a compilation of tangible examples of courses taught in English by foreign language faculty, who have intentionally incorporated elements of a foreign language in their humanities course curriculum. In this way, foreign language faculty will be better positioned to attract new language learners from these courses into their foreign language classrooms.

Incorporating foreign language content in humanities courses – our approach

While many additional areas of content expertise exist among foreign language educators, this collection describes courses that are organized in three categories: literature, linguistics, and culture. Working within these categories, the project includes multiple languages – Chinese, French, German, Japanese, Portuguese, Spanish – taught at the university, directed at various levels, from elementary through advanced, in order to reach a broad audience. This project brings together concrete examples of a variety of foreign language-infused humanities courses, taught by a diverse group of language faculty at the undergraduate level. Replete with lesson plans, class activities, assessment procedures, and the like, laid out in a ready-to-use format that any foreign language teacher can easily adapt and use, this volume is invaluable for those who would like to include foreign language content in their courses. The key is that this volume offers a useful guide to all foreign language faculty, without regard to their language specialty, for the adaptation and development of their own curricula that incorporates foreign language content into English-taught humanities courses.

Contained in this volume is a plethora of ways to highlight foreign language content for students in a way that peaks their interest and allows them to see the connection between foreign languages and other content that interests them, be it literature, linguistics, or culture. These ideas are organized in a way that provides parallel information to the reader. Contributors to this volume prepared chapters based on a template that included essential information pertaining to their courses. In addition to general information about the type of course being offered and the foreign languages highlighted within the course, contributors provide a description of the topic on which their course was built in a section called "Contextualization of Topic." "Course Logistics," including information such as credit hours, schedule, what type of requirements the course fulfills and any prerequisites attached to the course, may also be found in each chapter. The contributors further present the course objectives and learning outcomes for their courses. In the "Curricular Structure" section, the approach to designing the course is given, as well as the grade composition for the course. The "Theoretical Framework" section describes the pedagogical and theoretical components that were used to construct the course and its content. The "Teaching Materials," "Class Activities," "Ideas for Future Class Activities," and "Evaluation" sections are included in each chapter to illustrate core assignments and their grading criteria, which usually represent summative assessments for the course. When available, "Student Feedback" pertaining to the language content of the course is also provided. Finally, in the "Caveats and Reflections" section, contributors have the opportunity to reflect on the strengths and weaknesses of the course and its content, as well as the use of foreign languages within the course. Following a parallel format to increase accessibility for the reader, the contributors to this edited volume offer myriad strategies undertaken by foreign language faculty at the undergraduate level to incorporate the target language (e.g., Chinese, French, Japanese, Portuguese, and Spanish) into humanities content courses taught in English. Part I of this collection examines the incorporation of language content in literature courses. In the opening chapter, "Linking Language and Literature," Lyons explores foreign literature in translation examined through the lens of "Crazy Love." Her study of global literature provides a tremendous opportunity to expose students to words, phrases, and other aspects of foreign languages drawn from texts originally written in French, German, Italian, Japanese, and Spanish. In the second chapter, "A Bilingual Approach to a Humanities Course: Enriching Japanese Learning through Translating Flash Fiction into English," Ryu offers an innovative approach to enhancing cultural literacy and literary study. Ryu elucidates ways to utilize translation of flash fiction, a subgenre of Japanese literature that includes "cell phone novels" and "twitterature," to teach cultural and literary studies. Next, Huntington's "Engaging Language Policies and Poetics in an African Literature Classroom," brings French language and some indigenous African languages into focus through a translingual course that engages multiliteracies pedagogies. Huntington offers strategies for language learning through themes that connect language and identity as negotiated in political and practical spaces. Chapter four, "Finding Meaning in Translation: Critical Reading for Japanese Literature and Film in Translation," presents Takagi's strategies for bringing authenticity to the English translation of Japanese literature by exposing students to the subtleties and nuances of original texts and Japanese language films. Takagi focuses on women's position in Japanese society through literature and film, using a historical lens. The last chapter of Part I is "Spanish Golden Age Literature in the General Education Curriculum: Sharing the Riches of Culture and Language." In this chapter, Kalinoski offers ways to present material in a bilingual format to promote language learning through the study of literature and culture of the Spanish Golden Age, including drama and novels, essays, and film.

In Part II, this volume highlights innovative linguistics courses that engage students in language learning. Ananth's "Japanese and English in Contact: Linguistic and Cultural Perspectives" explores the influence that English and Japanese language have on each other as manifested in advertising, print media, and J-pop. Ananth's chapter offers concrete ideas about how to conceive of, prepare for, and execute a sociolinguistics course that is attractive to an audience that may not have any previous language background. Chapter seven, Negrelli's "Understanding Key Sociocultural Concepts in Japanese: Unlocking the Door to Communication," presents a course that prepares students for a meaningful short-term study abroad program by examining representative terms, key cultural concepts, and sociocultural aspects in the Japanese language that provide an insight into the social hierarchy. Next, Ito highlights major sociocultural aspects of language use in Japan through her chapter, "Approaching Language Issues Critically: Language in Japanese Society." Her course examines writing systems, loan words, regional dialects, and gender differences in Japanese language to reveal a nuanced perspective on Japanese society. In Chapter nine, Sugimori presents Reacting to the Past as a methodology for introducing students to the impact of the historical Japanese language policy on modern orthographic systems. Moreover, her chapter "Japanese Sociolinguistics: Reacting to the Past and Beyond," offers multiple ways to raise students' awareness of communication style differences in English and Japanese. The next chapter, Ueno's "Language, Identity, and Power in Japan: Gender in Japanese Language" explores Japanese language use as a manifestation of social and cultural identity through social attributes such as gender, status, age, and degree of intimacy. Ueno's chapter discusses ways to analyze gendered identities in Japanese language through the examination of honorifics, sexist language, and girl-graphs.

Finally, Part III presents examples of the infusion of foreign language content in humanities courses that focus on culture. Tashiro's "Teaching *Katakana* in a Cool Japan Culture Course" is the lead chapter of this section. It examines the use of *katakana*, a type of Japanese script, through various aspects of Japanese popular culture such as food, technology, cute culture, and religious practices. In Chapter twelve, "Understanding Chinese Behavioral Culture through Cross-cultural Communication," Jia presents behavioral culture as a significant aspect of foreign language education. In her course, complex cultural behavior is used as a means to expose students to foreign language content. Nogueira weaves language elements into her interdisciplinary culture course as described in her chapter, "Introducing the Portuguese Language through Brazilian Popular Culture." Highlighting the relationship of knowledge across disciplines, Nogueira discusses the use of language in such topics from Carnival to Capoeira. In Chapter fourteen, "Culture and Language Appreciation in a History of Latin America Course," Glick offers ways to include vocabulary, grammar, and culture from three foreign languages in an online survey course on the history of Latin America. Topics including race and gender are scrutinized through the examination of language in this engaging course. Finally, Trotman illuminates Spanish language and Hispanic culture through myth and legend from creation myths to concepts of the afterlife in her chapter "Heroes and Heroínas: Teaching Myths and Legends through Hispanic Culture." Students are afforded the opportunity to reflect on the notion of cultural identity while gaining exposure to Spanish language concepts.

This edited volume provides an array of exciting courses being taught in English that contain foreign language content. Offering such courses is a strategy for increasing foreign language enrollments by reaching a target audience of students who may have little or no previous experience with foreign language learning. This volume provides an important pedagogical resource to stimulate foreign language faculty to effect curricular changes and innovations in their classrooms. Such changes will promote the relationship between foreign language and humanities content to appeal to new language learners and motivate continuing language learners to remain committed to language studies.

References

Allen, Wendy, et al. "Foreign Languages across the Curriculum: The Applied Foreign Language Component." *Foreign Language Annals*, vol. 25, 1992, pp. 11–19.

Bettencourt, Michelle. "Languages across the Curriculum: A Response to Internationalization in Foreign Language Education." *Multicultural Education*, vol. 19, no. 1, 2011, pp. 55–58.

Brinton, Donna M., et al. *Content-Based Second Language Instruction*. University of Michigan Press, 2003.

Caldwell, Marie Ann. "A FLAC Model for Increasing Enrollment in Foreign Language Classes." *The French Review: Special Issue on Pedagogy*, vol. 74, no. 6, 2001, pp. 1125–1137.

Geisler, Michael, et al. "Foreign Languages and Higher Education: New Structures for a Changed World: MLA Ad Hoc Committee on Foreign Languages." *Profession*, 2007, pp. 234–245. JSTOR, www.jstor.org/stable/25595871.

Humanities Departmental Surveys, 2007–2008. *The American Academy of Arts and Sciences*. humanitiesindicators.org/binaries/pdf/humanitiesDepartmentalSurvey.pdf. Accessed 30 April 2019.

Humanities Departmental Surveys, 2012–2013. *The American Academy of Arts and Sciences*. humanitiesindicators.org/content/indicatordoc.aspx?i=457. Accessed 30 April 2019.

Johnson, Steven. "Colleges Lose a 'Stunning' 651 Foreign-Language Programs in 3 Years." *The Chronicle of Higher Education*. 22 Jan. 2019. www.chronicle.com/article/Colleges-Lose-a-Stunning-/245526. Accessed 28 April 2019.

Jurasek, Richard. "Integrating Foreign Languages into the College Curriculum." *The Modern Language Journal*, vol. 72, no. 1, 1988, pp. 52–58.

Karsen, Sonja. "Literature in Translation: Trend or Necessity?" *Fourth International Conference of OMLTA and NYSAFLT*, 1975. pp. 3–10. files.eric.ed.gov/fulltext/ED104164.pdf. Web.

Looney, Dennis, and Natalia Lusin. "Enrollments in Languages Other Than English in United States Institutions of Higher Education," *Summer 2016 and Fall 2016: Preliminary Report*. MLA Publications, 2018.

Mignolo, Walter D. "The Role of the Humanities in the Corporate University." *PMLA*, vol. 115, no. 5, 2000, pp. 1238–1245. *JSTOR*, www.jstor.org/stable/463306.

Spinelli, Emily. "Languages across the Curriculum: A Postsecondary Initiative." *HOW Journal*, vol. 3, no. 1, 1998, pp. 13–18.

Zakaria, Fareed. *In Defense of a Liberal Education*. W.W. Norton & Company, 2015.

Part I
Literature

1 Linking language and literature

Leah Tolbert Lyons

Course Title: HUM 2610 Foreign Literature in Translation: "Crazy Love"
Course Level: Sophomore
Language(s) in Focus: Spanish, German, French, Italian, Japanese
Course Type: Humanities, Literature

Contextualization of topic

"Foreign Literature in Translation" is the general topic for the course. As the topic suggests, the course involves the study of literature that has been translated from its original language into English. While this topic is well suited for a course designed to provide students with access to world literatures with which they might not otherwise engage, it is also impersonal and insufficiently descriptive to attract students and give them any sense of how the course might be of specific interest to them personally. With this in mind, I added the subtopic "Crazy Love" to the course. "Crazy Love" has a measure of universality, since the notion of romantic love, often with its attendant dysfunction and heartache, has been the subject of artistic works through the ages.

Course logistics

This 3-credit-hour course meets twice weekly for 85 min. The course satisfies a Humanities/Fine Arts General Education requirement but may also be taken for elective credit. There are no foreign language prerequisites placed on the course; rather, the prerequisites include first-year English composition courses. Designed for on-campus, face-to-face teaching, this course is the recommended Humanities/Fine Arts General Education course for Foreign Language majors.

Course objectives

The following course objective was established for "Crazy Love":

> The goal of Humanities 2610, Foreign Literature in Translation: "Crazy Love" is to help students develop an appreciation of literature that stems from a cultural context that is different from one's own while expanding global perspectives and challenging the individual's worldview.

Learning outcomes

The course objective is tied to the following learning outcomes. Upon completion of this course, the successful student will be able to

- Analyze primary texts as a form of cultural and creative expression
- Understand how the texts express the culture and values of their time and place
- Explore global/cultural diversity
- Understand critical and analytical methodologies for literary analysis
- Develop integrative/reflective thinking by making connections across multiple contexts and educational experiences

Curricular structure

The course requirements emanate from the course objectives and student learning outcomes. Much attention was paid to establishing requirements that would allow students to demonstrate the skills they were developing throughout the course and the knowledge they had gained.

Grade Composition:

(20%) Class Participation: Students must discuss the required readings in depth and thus contribute to a positive learning environment where each student is respected and the exchange of ideas is valued.

(45%) Quizzes: Reading quizzes (approximately 19) are administered for each reading assignment given. The quizzes consist of 5–10 straightforward questions to assess reading comprehension and motivate students to stay current in their reading.

(15%) Group Project: Working in groups (4–6 students), but graded individually, students complete a multimedia project based on one of the suggestions below:
- "Crazy Love" Mix Tape—students will identify at least six love songs that match the readings for the course and present them on CD with cover art and liner notes that include complete song lyrics and a thorough examination of their connection to the readings.
- "Crazy Love" Mock-u-Drama—students will write, perform, and record a play/skit with a plot composed of elements from each of the course readings.
- "Crazy Love" Morning News—students will create a newspaper consisting of a feature story, an editorial, an advice column (at least two questions and answers), cartoon, and several want ads, based on various events that occur among the course readings.

In addition to the final product, students submit three forms (planning, peer assessment, and self-assessment), as well as a reflection paper to comment on the process of completing the group project.

(20%) Essay: A combination argumentative essay/response paper, students write an essay manifesting the interconnectedness of the required course material through literary analysis, as well as discuss how the course has impacted their personal development and academic progress.

Theoretical framework

Since each text students read shares a common theme, the approach to the course is thematic in nature. Given the task of literary analysis that the course requires, it is important to introduce students to various forms of literary criticism. Fairly accessible to undergraduate students, the historical approach, postcolonial theory, and feminist theory are typically mentioned at some point during the classroom discussions. In its examination of literature, the course is anchored in reader-response theory. Like Roland Barthes in his essay "The Death of the Author," the approach to the course mitigates the role of the author and emphasizes the reader as the key component to the construction of meaning in the text. It is the use of language and the reader's interpretation thereof that allow for the construction of the literary work of art. Regarding the theoretical approach to the class meetings themselves, as a discussion-based course, the design of the class draws loosely on Gordon Pask's Conversation Theory. It moves easily between the three levels of conversation that the theory prescribes, from general discussion to specific subject matter and the use of metalanguage pertaining to that subject matter.

Teaching materials

Several fiction texts are used in the course. Literature is to be read individually and discussed in class. The film is to be viewed outside the class and may be done individually or in groups organized by the students themselves based on their schedules and availability. The current reading list and film options are as follows, in order of scheduled reading:

Required readings

- *Like Water for Chocolate: A Novel in Monthly Installments with Recipes, Romances, and Home Remedies*, Laura Esquivel, translated by Carol Christensen and Thomas Christensen, 1992
- *A Sad Affair*, Wolfgang Koeppen, translated by Michael Hofmann, 2003
- *Contempt*, Alberto Moravia, translated by Angus Davidson, 1999
- *Scarlet Song*, Mariama Bâ, translated by Dorothy S. Blair, 1994
- *Love Suicide at Amijima*, Monzaemon Chikamatsu, translated by Asataro Miyamori, 2000
- *The Swallows of Kabul*, Yasmina Khadra, translated by John Cullen, 2004

Required film

- *Like Water for Chocolate*, Alfonso Arau, 1992
  OR
- *Contempt*, Jean-Luc Godard, 1963

Class activities

Since it is discussion-based, the course relies almost exclusively on some form of classroom discussion in each meeting. Here is an example of a typical lesson plan for an 85 min. class, with variations provided below.

- (5 min.) General conversation and announcements
- (20–25 min.) Reading quiz

Linking language and literature 19

- (50–55 min.) Full-class discussion, small group conversations, visual representation of literary work, or debate
- (5 min.) Concluding comments and preview of the next class

The format for full-class discussions roughly mimics the stages of conversation outlined in Pask's Conversation Theory.

- Natural Language (for basic conversation): An opening question such as "What do you think of this book?" typically elicits basic comments on students' likes/dislikes, the difficulty level of the reading, and the like. Among these comments, there are usually some that pertain to plot and characters. From there, more detailed questions emerge.
- Object Language (for a given topic of conversation): At this point we begin to discuss the book in more in-depth terms, perhaps looking at specific passages or citing specific scenes to illustrate a point or opinion.
- Metalanguage (for clarifying a certain topic): To address critical thinking, we employ the metalanguage of English, using more discrete literary terms to think critically about the text. We begin to discuss the themes and the techniques and devices used to support those themes. It is often at this point that questions of language/translation arise. There are phrases in the various literatures that represent idiom, hyperbole, metaphor, etc., which beg closer attention. Examining these increases comprehension, reveals the importance of foreign language content, and raises cultural awareness.

Variations to full-class discussions

- Small Group Conversations: Especially if at least one student is noticeably shy and reticent to participate in the full-class discussion, students may be arranged in groups of 3–5 to begin discussing the reading assignment before combining into a larger group. The small group conversations are not guided by the instructor. Once conversation begins, the instructor moves about the room to check in with the various groups and answer questions as needed.
- Visual Representation of the Literary Work: Students work in groups (according to class size and available materials— whiteboard space and markers) to give a visual representation of the Japanese play *Love Suicide at Amijima*. While this activity

could be applied to other texts, the play's brevity and three-part structure make it ideal for this activity. The students are told to "create a visual representation of the play," having been advised that no artistic ability is needed to complete the task, informed that everyone must participate in the process, and cautioned that no words or symbols should be used. (Although on occasion, students who have studied Japanese language are granted permission to write a caption in Japanese.) The product is often a series of images that depict the main events of the plot. Sometimes students construct diagrams or other images that represent the concepts expressed in the play. Once the students have worked together to create the visual representation, they explain what they have done for the class, which undoubtedly leads to a discussion of the importance of language, as students have either been denied access to written language and symbols for this activity or written in a foreign language.

- Debate: Usually centered on an issue such as polygamy, domestic violence, or infidelity, the class is divided in half to determine which side of the argument the group will represent, and then in half again to allow for smaller discussion groups to identify their arguments. Both sides regroup to form two teams for a debate-style discussion with arguments and rebuttals that rely on textual evidence.

Examples of language content discussion topics

- ➢ *Como agua para chocolate (Like water for chocolate)* is a phrase that is frequently discussed, not only because it is the original title of the literary work students read but also because it is a line of the novel used to describe the main character's mental state. Students' curiosity about the fact that a line in the book mirrors the title provides the opportunity for a foray into foreign language discussion. On several occasions, I have had students who have familiarity with the novel in the original language from past language classes. Discussion of the Spanish language gives the opportunity for students to "teach" other students, allowing for greater comprehension and retention. This may also spark further interest in foreign languages and provides the opportunity to ask students if they have knowledge of similar expressions in their own and other languages.

Linking language and literature 21

➤ *Eine unglückliche Liebe*, the title of the novel by Wolfgang Koeppen, has been translated into English as *A Sad Affair*. We examine the word *unglückliche* and its possible translation into English as "unrequited" when referring to love. We discuss the potential ways the interpretation of the novel would differ if the title of the novel were different.

➤ In the novel, *A Sad Affair*, there is a comical scene where the main character, Friedrich, meets his love interest for the first time. Overwhelmed by her beauty and the fact that there is a girl in his shabby room, Friedrich is unsure whether to use the formal register or the informal register to greet her. The German expressions that the character uses are not translated, since there would be no indication of register in the English translation. Consequently, students often overlook the humor in the scene because they fail to understand that even basic facility in his native language is thrown into chaos by the mere presence of a beautiful woman. This scene and the German phrases used provide an excellent opportunity to examine foreign language content in the classroom.

➤ The novel *Scarlet Song* provides opportunities to discuss foreign language content because there are untranslated words in the text that are found in a glossary. Even though the untranslated words are in Wolof, a language that is not offered at our university, they provide an opportunity for the students to engage with the author's choice to not include those words or phrases in French language (and hence in English language translation). In the novel, language is a barrier that separates various characters, as evidenced by the use of the untranslated word *toubab*, for example, a name for white people used in West Africa. The intentional choice of language used (and what remains untranslated) is a way to leverage power. Acknowledging this use of language in the text can lead to a philosophical discussion of the political implication of former French colonial subjects publishing in a colonial language, a longstanding discussion in the field of postcolonial theory.

➤ In *The Swallows of Kabul*, several words and phrases appear in the text in Arabic, even though the novel was originally published in French. The use of Arabic words and phrases provide a cultural point of reference for the reader. For example, the Islamic phrase *Allahu akbar* ("God is greater") is a common phrase used in the Muslim world, but is sometimes wrongly associated in the West with terrorist activity. While focusing on the use of a foreign language, students are also encouraged to discuss stereotypes and biases that, once debunked, allow students to better relate to the characters they are reading and accomplish higher order thinking about social questions the students may face on campus and beyond.

➢ In the assigned foreign language films *Like Water for Chocolate* and *Contempt*, there is an opening to expose students to foreign language content, albeit outside of the classroom. *Like Water for Chocolate* is in Spanish and allows students to hear the original language of the novel. In class, I underscore the interesting interpretation of Alberto Moravia's Italian novel *Contempt* by French filmmaker Jean-Luc Godard because it focuses on miscommunication and language. The Italian protagonists are cast as French people living in Italy, working on a film produced by an American, and directed by a German, legendary filmmaker Fritz Lang. This film adaptation gives students the opportunity to hear several foreign languages.

Ideas for future class activities

While in the past, entire films have been screened in class, time constraints have prevented this practice from continuing. With the rise of streaming video accessibility, in the future, shorter film excerpts may be viewed in class so foreign language may be heard in the classroom. Discussion of the film excerpts may be based on the following:

- Visual cues for cultural communication associated with language
- The suitability and sufficiency of subtitling

Evaluation

While formative assessments such as reading comprehension quizzes are a great way to assess the students' attainment of the plot outlines and character development in fictional works, it is in the classroom discussions where critical thinking is applied from class session to class session. When constantly asked to think about their opinions and justify them not only with the texts being read but also with real-life scenarios, student development is ascertainable. The manifestation of critical thinking is seen in the summative assessments: the group project and the essay that synthesizes the course material. In order to determine potential essay topics, students work in groups to brainstorm. While unfortunately, some groups begin their discussion trying to determine what the professor "wants" them to write about, others begin to look thematically at the literature to find commonalities and to group ideas together.

Here are some examples of general essay topics students discover:

- Discuss the gender roles in the texts.
- What are the contributing factors to the decline of the marital/romantic relationship?
- Discuss the role of communication in the romantic relationships.
- How does the notion of family impact the characters' decisions and the outcomes of those decisions?

Caveats and reflections

The strength of the course rests on the students and their engagement with the literature through in-depth discussion that develops critical thinking. A weakness of the course is that it relies almost exclusively on the students' willingness to engage with the material. They must read consistently and participate in class discussions, making an investment in the work of critical thinking. Over the years, students have successfully accomplished this task again and again. The course contributes to the mandate of higher education to help students acquire the requisite knowledge and skills to contribute positively to our ever-changing world. "Crazy Love" is a deeply satisfying course because it provides an opportunity to link language and literature for students in a way that exposes them to two academic fields that they may otherwise not pursue. By incorporating language content in the course, students have an increased awareness of the role language plays in their daily lives.

References

Barthes, Roland. "The Death of the Author." *Image, Music, Text*, edited by Stephen Heath. Fontana Press, 1977, pp. 142–148, PDF.
"Conversation Theory (Gordon Pask)." InstructionalDesign.org, www.instructionaldesign.org/theories/conversation-theory.
Pask, Gordon. *Conversation, Cognition and Learning: A Cybernetic Theory and Methodology*. Elsevier, 1975.

Teaching material references

Bâ, Mariama. *Scarlet Song*. Translated by Dorothy S. Blair, Longman, 1986.
Chikamatsu, *Love Suicide at Amijima*. Translated by Asataro Miyamori, In Parenthesis Publications, 2000, PDF.

Contempt. Directed by Jean-Luc Godard, COCINOR, 1963.
Esquivel, Laura. *Like Water for Chocolate: A Novel in Monthly Installments with Recipes, Romances, and Home Remedies.* Translated by Carol Christensen and Thomas Christensen, Doubleday, 1992.
Khadra, Yasmina. *The Swallows of Kabul.* Translated by John Cullen, Doubleday, 2004.
Koeppen, Wolfgang. *A Sad Affair.* Translated by Michael Hofmann, W.W. Norton & Company, 2003.
Like Water for Chocolate. Directed by Alfonso Arau, Miramax, 1992.
Moravia, Alberto. *Contempt.* Translated by Angus Davidson, New York Review of Books, 1999.

2 A bilingual approach to a humanities course: enriching Japanese learning through translating flash fiction into English

Catherine Ryu

Course Title: JPN 469: Japanese Cultural and Literary Studies II on Flash Fiction, Japanese Culture and Translation
Course Level: Upper-Division
Language(s) in Focus: Japanese
Course Type: Japanese Studies, Culture, Literature

Contextualization of topic

This course focuses on a literary genre known as "flash fiction" as a lens through which Japanese culture is explored. This genre encompasses a variety of writings that share brevity as their defining characteristic. While flash fiction is a recent global phenomenon facilitated by digital technologies, it is by no means a new form of writing in the Japanese literary tradition. This course cultivates students' understanding of six subgenres of flash fiction in Japanese and the ways they are connected:

- Contemporary *tanka* ("short poem" with 31 syllables), a precursor to *haiku*
- Traditional *tanka*
- Contemporary *haiku*
- "Twitterature" (micro novels using tweets)
- *Keitai* (cell phone) novels
- *Uta monogatari* (poem-tale narratives)

Course logistics

This is a 3-credit-hour course offered twice a week for 80 min. per session. This course fulfills a writing requirement for Japanese majors and has as its prerequisites JPN369 (Japanese Cultural and Literary Studies I) and three years of Japanese (intermediate proficiency) or its equivalent.

Course objectives

- Analytical Thinking: The ability to analyze primary sources by learning to recognize frequently used poetic and narrative patterns of thought and expression
- Integrated Reasoning: The ability to integrate the analysis of primary sources to yield a meaningful thematic interpretation in their original linguistic, cultural, and historical contexts
- Effective Communication: The ability to express persuasively and logically in English an interpretation of primary sources based on an informed understanding of the Japanese literary tradition and the Japanese language
- Intercultural Understanding: An informed understanding of flash fiction in Japanese and its intersections with digital writing in global contexts

Learning outcomes

Students will demonstrate attainment of the course objectives through the creation of a digital portfolio. The concrete outcome of the coursework is a mini-anthology of flash fiction in Japanese compiled by each student at the end of the term as his or her final course project. This bilingual anthology, showcased as a website, serves as a space for demonstrating each student's aggregate learning over 15 weeks. While the website itself is not graded, it functions as a digital portfolio, including a student's profile and translation approach developed throughout the term. The website also features a brief introduction to each subgenre of flash fiction covered in the course; critical analysis of chosen samples from all subgenres, noting cultural and linguistic grammars pertinent to the Japanese original; audio files of the primary sources (in Japanese); and a list of references.

Curricular structure

The curricular approach employed for the course is backward design. To assist students in developing their website contents, subgenres of flash fiction are introduced in the order of accessibility (from high to low) in terms of content, language, literary genre, and length, while scaffolding subgenres (poetry and prose). The course thus begins with Tawara Machi's contemporary *tanka*, utilizing relatable themes (e.g., love, family, nature) and diction close to everyday speech. After having explored *haiku*, classical *tanka*, twitterature, and cell phone novels, it ends with *The Tales of Ise*, a celebrated work belonging to a hybrid genre of poem-tale from the 10th century. The evaluation criteria are correlated to six learning activities across all modules:

(10%) Quizzes
(30%) In-class participation
(24%) Online assignment
(15%) Module reports
(5%) Micro-presentations
(16%) Final course project

Whereas quizzes on secondary sources are assessed based on accuracy, other learning activities on primary sources are based mainly on students' preparedness, measured in terms of thoroughness and timely submissions of all required materials, and by the level of their engagement during in-class activities. For all online assignments, including module reports, micro-presentations, and the final course projects, students are provided with templates. The use of templates facilitates the evaluation in three ways:

- To measure the degree of each assignment's completeness and thoroughness by individual students
- To assess the overall progress of students collectively and identify challenges that need to be addressed with the class as a whole, while allowing students to self-evaluate their own work through pair work and group discussion
- To enable all members to learn translation as a system involving multiple steps, including articulating rationales for modifications in the edits made to each draft

Theoretical framework

Conceived as a project-based course, each session functions as a hands-on workshop comprised of two parts: Part I focuses on discussing submitted online assignments, whereas Part II prepares students to complete the next assignment, including a group translation activity through which the class produces a rough draft of a sample work from the next target genre. In such a way, the workshop format is operationalized through streamlined task-based activities and assignments.

Teaching materials

No textbooks are required for the course. Required course materials are available through an online course management system. All teaching materials are open online sources, as well as published materials with authors' permission. Sample teaching materials include the following. Additional materials can be found in the References section.

- "Flash Fiction East," Myfanway Collins, 2009
- "Machi no hitori hyakushû," Tawara Machi, 2002

Class activities

This sample lesson plan is for the second session on the twitterature module. This module is designed to demonstrate how the use of Twitter with an absolute character limit brings out the fundamental and functional differences in Japanese and English as written languages. This in turn invites students to think deeply and creatively about how to negotiate noted differences in the original tweet in Japanese and their own English translation specifically as illustrations of a subgenre in flash fiction.

- (5 min.) Review of the official trailer of 無人地帯 (Mujin Chitai. *No Man's Zone*, documentary, 2012) and *haiku* focused on 3.11 (a triple disaster that happened in Japan in 2011) from the previous session
- (5 min.) Class discussions: "What's in a hashtag (#twnovel)?" and "What does it mean to focus on 3.11 as a topic for twitterature (140 字の物語: a 140-character story) in contrast to a documentary and *haiku*?"
- (2 min.) Introduction of the class tweet:
  神様が、貧しい親子に僅かなお金を与えました。親子はそのお金で、パンを買いました。パン屋は、パンを売って鞄を買いました。鞄屋は、鞄を売って家具を買いました。家具屋は、家具を売って馬を買いました。馬を持っているお金持ちは、困っている人々のために、パンを買いました。
  @yukiririkiriri #twnovel 19 March 2011, 16:38:09. Tweet.
- (2 min.) Group recitations of the class tweet
- (6 min.) Class Discussion: Linguistic analysis of the class tweet based on patterns of nouns and verbs therein:

  Nouns: 神様, 親子, お金, パン, パン屋, 鞄, 鞄屋, 家具, 家具屋, 馬, お金持ち, 人々, ため
  Verbs: 与えました, 買いました, 持っている, 困っている

A POS (parts of speech) analysis, output of the tweet and a frequency list by Auto-Parser (http://tool.konisimple.net/text/hinshi_keitaiso), and its significance

> Example: the most frequently used verb: 買いました [to buy, past tense, neutral polite] appears five times in this tweet, pointing to the importance of purchasing power in times of disaster, as well as how to meet basic needs for physical survival

- (6 min.) Class discussion: thematic analysis of the class tweet

  > Example: the socioeconomic significance of this 3.11-focused tweet reflected in the chain of nouns in the order of お金 (money), パン (bread), 鞄 (bags), 家具 (furniture), 馬 (horse), and back to パン (bread)

- (8 min.) Group translation of the class tweet through an error analysis of machine translations by Google Translate and Weblio
- (6 min.) Class discussion of the class tweet in light of cultural, social, and literary references

  > Example: how to determine English equivalents of such a term as 神様 (god or gods, Shinto deity or deities, or retain the original "kami") so as to reflect the cultural textures and nuances of the original Japanese term and to maintain the overall tone and diction of the Japanese original with its fairytale-like overtones

- (10 min.) Pair work on the analysis of student #twnovels prepared for the session
- (10 min.) Group work: reduce the number of characters in the English translation of the class tweet and analyze the challenges this task poses
- (10 min.) Group work: do the same for students' translations of their own #twnovel
- (5 min.) Class discussion: merits and demerits of maintaining the 140-word limit in English translations of Japanese tweets
- (5 min.) Introduction to the next assignment: completing an article review template for the assigned article on twitterature and revising individual and class tweets

Ideas for future class activities

One idea for future class activities is a three-minute podcast recording. Prior to this activity, students submit a proposal including a topic to be covered (any aspect of flash fiction covered in the course), guests (if any), questions to be asked, and a rationale for the proposed podcast. This activity offers an additional opportunity for students to reflect on their learning experience, while augmenting the website for their future career or advanced academic training, as well as familiarizing themselves with available digital tools for knowledge production, curation, and dissemination.

Evaluation

Formative tools

Assignment templates constitute a key formative tool. While each template is tailored to address specific attributes of a subgenre of flash fiction, common features across modules include a chosen primary source written out in *hiragana* Japanese to ensure the accuracy of students' reading comprehension; two machine translations of the primary source and a comparative error analysis; students' own translations of the primary source, including specific translation challenges; how they resolved prior challenges; students' comparative analysis of their own translations and published translations by professionals. In-class participation is another key formative tool with which students learn the course materials and contribute to in-class activities, such as pair work, group discussion, and class discussion, as well as dramatic reading of the original in Japanese and its English translation. Quizzes function as yet another formative tool with which to assess students' grasp of the secondary sources, indispensable for enhancing their understanding of historical and cultural aspects of the primary sources for each module. This understanding serves as the basis for drafting an informed introduction to each subgenre of flash fiction in Japanese for the final website project.

Summative tools

The module report submitted at the end of each module functions as a summative tool. For this assignment, students revise and polish their translations of the primary sources, thereby deepening their understanding of Japanese culture through their translation of flash fiction. One critical aspect of summative evaluation is the timing of the instructor's feedback. In addition to oral feedback during class, the instructor's written comments (usually on the second draft of students' translation and module reports) are meant to encourage the ability of students to think, self-assess, and develop a translation that is truly their own. Students are, however, required to explain their translation decisions in relation to the instructor's feedback.

The micro-presentation is utilized as another summative tool with which students can polish the art of presentation based on their completed module reports. Moreover, this time-bound exercise (5 min.) enhances students' ability to assess the most essential aspect of their module reports.

The final project is the ultimate summative tool. By successfully completing this project, students demonstrate their deepened understanding of the six forms of flash fiction in Japanese covered in the course.

Samples of the final projects from JPN469 include

- https://mccormicklily.wixsite.com/lilymtranslations
- https://gagnons2.wixsite.com/jpn469-portfolio/references
- https://liechenstien.wixsite.com/mysite

Student feedback

Below is qualitative student feedback excerpted from their translation approaches articulated at the end of the term:

- "As a non-native speaker of Japanese, I often struggle with comprehending [such] nominalization. To combat this weakness, I drew up a diagram of how the child is nominalized during my linguistic analysis. Viewing the diagram makes it clear how the child is modified by explicitly showing where this takes place in the original Japanese and how we can interpret in English as it is in my final draft."
- "In essence, I have found that the process of translation is not so much illustrated with the idea of a simple exhalation to restore artistic flair and context to a piece, as much as it is constructing a mechanical breathing apparatus with tools through many rounds of trial and error interspersed with design team consultations."
- "As much as you know about the language going into translation, you are constantly learning through the original author as each author writes with a different purpose. Translation is not about changing words, but bridging people and cultures, which you can only learn one word at a time."

Caveats and reflections

One challenge of the course is the intense intellectual engagement with the course materials required over 15 weeks. Optimal learning happens when all members are fully prepared for each session. However, for those without a sufficient level of language proficiencies (whether in English or Japanese), as well as those without good study habits, this course can be rather challenging. For the instructor, this course is labor intensive. Since each student chooses different samples from the primary sources, the instructor needs to provide individualized feedback in a timely fashion. In the current semester, the number of enrolled students doubled (18 compared to 9 in the previous year). To maintain the quality of students' work and learning, the instructor reduced the number of works translated in each subgenre. To compensate for that, students additionally adopt a class translation of the sample work chosen by the instructor; personalize it; and share it with each other. The weakness thus identified can be the strength of the course as well, since it encourages the students to learn from each other's work.

One of the benefits of this course with a bilingual approach to flash fiction is that it enhances "metalinguistic awareness" (Cazden). By constantly working between Japanese and English, students gain a nuanced understanding of how each language works. At the same time, the reiterative process of translation in concert with ongoing self-reflection on the act of translation allows students to increase their metacognitive awareness of how their own learning takes place (Kemp, Adescope et al.). Moreover, a bilingual approach enables students to gain a greater degree of intercultural understanding and effective communication through the step-by-step process of translation practices and assessments. Furthermore, students can acquire a higher level of analytical and problem-solving skills by working through translation challenges, linguistically and culturally. JPN469 as a translation-focused humanities course thus contributes to equipping students with enhanced cross-linguistic proficiency, together with a keen intercultural understanding in global contexts facilitated by swiftly changing digital technologies.

References

Adescope, Olusola O., et al. "A Systematic Review and Meta-analysis of Cognitive Correlates of Bilingualism." *Review of Educational Research*, vol. 80, no. 2, 2010, pp. 207–245.

Cazden, Courtney B. "Play with Language and Metalinguistic Awareness: One Dimension of Language Experience." *Urban Review*, vol. 7, 1974, pp. 28–29.

Kemp, Charlotte. "Strategic Processing in Grammar Learning: Do Multilinguals Use More Strategies?" *International Journal of Bilingualism*, vol. 4, 2007, pp. 241–261.

Teaching material references

Collins, Myfanway. "Flash Fiction East." *American Book Review*, vol. 30, no. 3, March/April 2009, p. 26.

Hansen, Kelly. "Electronic Literature and Youth Culture: The Rise of the Japanese Cell Phone Novel." *Routledge Handbook of Modern Literature*, edited by Rachel Hutchinson and Leith Douglas Morton. Routledge, 2016, pp. 301–314.

Mika. *Koizora: setsunai koi monogatari*. Mahō no i-rando, 2005. s.maho.jp/book/af5770e0601598ef/6960568627. Accessed 1 April 2019.

Naito, Mika. *3/11 Kokoro ni nokoru 140-ji no monogatari*. Togetter, togetter.com/li/113436. Accessed 1 April 2019.

Ogura Hyakunin Isshu: 100 Poems by 100 Poets, 1998. jti.lib.virginia.edu/japanese/hyakunin/frames/hyakuframes.html. Accessed 1 April 2019.

Tawara, Machi. "Machi no hitori hyakushû," *Tawara Machi's Chocolate BOX*, 2002, gtpweb.net/twr/indexe.htm. Accessed 1 April 2019.

3 Engaging language policies and poetics in an African literature classroom

Julie Huntington

Course Title: EWL 365 Reading Contemporary Africa
Course Level: Advanced
Language(s) in Focus: French and additional languages including Akan, Baoulé, and Yoruba
Course Type: African Literature

Contextualization of topic

Literature courses with a broad regional focus can serve as adaptable, translingual offerings that support language learners and heritage speakers while introducing newcomers to the politics and poetics of one or more additional languages. In this Reading Contemporary Africa course, students work collaboratively across languages, texts, and contexts to cultivate a plurilingual classroom environment. In keeping with Chimamanda Ngozi Adichie's warnings about "The Danger of a Single Story," students learn to complicate and problematize the homogenizing and oversimplifying label *African*. Through their engagement with contemporary literary and cinematic works, students explore a multiplicity of linguistic themes including national language policies versus local language practices, the personalization and politicization of plurilingual expression, and the business and ethics of publication and translation.

Moreover, as students interact with creative works produced by Africa-based and Diasporic authors, they consider the importance and diversity of multiple intersecting elements (such as languages, histories, politics, economies, genders, sexualities, and sub/cultures) and support one another in developing multiliteracies. Offered as a manifesto by the New London Group in the 1990s, "A Pedagogy of Multiliteracies: Designing Social Futures" called for significant shifts in pedagogical philosophies and practices by redefining and expanding the concept of literacy education to include increased linguistic and cultural diversity and provide additional modes of technological communication and creative expression (63). A growing body of research in language education supports multiliteracies pedagogies in view of attaining the *World Readiness Standards for Learning Languages* and overcoming the language versus culture curricular divide denounced by the Modern Language Association. Beyond their effectiveness in language classes (see Paesani et al.), multiliteracies pedagogies offer important takeaways for students across academic disciplines. As Chantelle Warner and Beatrice Dupuy suggest: "Being an active designer of social futures involves developing a sense of agency and expression on one's own behalf. At the same time, it calls on a recognition on the part of learners and educators that the particular texts, contexts, and discourses with which we make meaning have an ethical dimension vis-à-vis others" (124). Indeed, multiliteracies pedagogies foster the development of the interpretive and analytical skillsets required to address complicated dimensions of positionality, relationality, and identity in local and global contexts.

Course logistics

This 3-credit-hour course in African literature is housed in the English and World Literatures department where it fulfills an upper-level elective requirement for the major as well as an upper-level General Education requirement.

Course objectives

In this course, students learn to

- Read contemporary African narratives with a deepened understanding of their historical, social, and cultural contexts
- Identify thematic and formal patterns in African fiction
- Design and conduct a research project on African narrative fiction

Learning outcomes

In this course, students demonstrate the ability to

- Interpret contemporary African narratives and articulate their understanding of how individual works reflect and/or refract the historical, social, and cultural contexts surrounding their production

- Prepare and present a mini-lesson on a theme that will expand classmates' comprehension of a given text or texts
- Develop, compose, and communicate a comparative research project in African narrative fiction

Curricular structure

The contemporary focus of this course best lends itself to a backward design approach. The selection and sequencing of course readings, activities, and assessments support learners as they work to achieve course objectives and demonstrate learning outcomes.

The overall grading breakdown is as follows:

(20%) Homework, Quizzes, and Cultural Activities
(20%) Midterm Exam
(10%) Mini Lesson
(40%) Research Presentation and Essay Portfolio
(10%) Active Class Participation

Theoretical framework

The building blocks for this course curriculum are broad thematic-based units including Stories and Storytelling, Multi-Local Identities, and Writing as Social Advocacy. For the final six weeks of the semester, the course shifts to a project-based focus, as students conduct independent research and prepare conference-length papers and presentations. In this translingual course, readings and assignments are designed for readers of two different primary languages—French and English—to maximize learning and engagement. Although most students complete their readings and assignments in English, in a given semester, 5%–15% of course enrollees opt for a dual-language curricular option.

In administering this type of translingual course, it is imperative to meet with dual-language option students to determine what types of assignments are level appropriate in accordance with ACTFL (American Council for the Teaching of Foreign Languages) or CEFR (Common European Framework of Reference for Languages) guidelines. Undoubtedly, working with individual students to design a dual-language curricular plan requires personalization and flexibility due to their potentially disparate degrees of linguistic proficiency. Whereas superior- and advanced-level students will be equipped to complete all of the requisite French-language tasks, students with lower or inconsistent proficiency levels require a scaled-back version of the French curricular track. For example, a student who demonstrates advanced-level reading but intermediate-level writing proficiencies will be capable of conducting readings and research in French, but might be ill-equipped to produce a sophisticated conference-length article. For these reasons, it is necessary to conduct the appropriate language assessments and agree upon a curricular plan that supports the student's demonstrated language proficiencies and learning goals.

Indeed, this move to promote plurilingualism in courses typically offered in English creates additional pathways for developing multiliteracies among learners. While the benefits of providing contexts and conditions for heritage speakers and language learners to broaden their knowledge and perspectives through level-appropriate activities in French are apparent, this translingual curricular model also presents English-track students with unique and expansive learning opportunities. As students engage in work across languages, they gain insight into how linguistic expression influences the ongoing processes of identity configuration and relational negotiation in a multiplicity of local and global contexts.

Teaching materials

Books

- *The Face: Cartography of the Void*, Chris Abani, 2016
- *What It Means When a Man Falls from the Sky*, Lesley Nneka Arimah, 2017
- *Homegoing*, Yaa Gyasi, 2016
- *Temps de chien*, Patrice Nganang, 2001 (In translation: *Dog Days*, Patrice Nganang, 2006)
- *Reine Pokou: Concerto pour un sacrifice*, Véronique Tadjo, 2005 (In translation: *Queen Pokou: Concerto for a Sacrifice*, Amy Baran Reid, 2009)

Films

- *The Wedding Party*, Kemi Adetiba, 2016
- *Welcome to Nollywood*, Jamie Meltzer, 2007
- *Timbuktu*, Abderrahmane Sissako, 2014

Class activities

The semester begins with a moment of comparative linguistics that invites students at all levels of language proficiency (from novice to distinguished) to participate in the work of translation and interpretation. After establishing a preliminary understanding of the power of linguistic frameworks, students move on to complete a series of activities that accentuate the plurilingual features of literary and cinematic works. As students attend to this series of tasks, they are encouraged to compare passages from the original and translated versions (when applicable), both in their small-group work and in dialogue with the class.

The following activities demonstrate how translingual objectives are achieved throughout the semester using a variety of modes of linguistic and literary analysis. The prompts are adaptable and can be completed as guided writing assignments or as interactive small-group activities:

➢ Overview: Language and Micro-level Translation, History versus Histoire
This activity is designed to be completed in the first or second class session to explore how languages frame knowledge, perspectives, and experiences.
Compare the terms "History" in English and *Histoire* in French. How are these words defined in monolingual and bilingual dictionaries? What are other ways of interpreting these two terms? Explain their significance. Next, consider how the concept of History/Histoire is expressed in other languages you are familiar with. Identify points of congruity and incongruity with your comparisons. Discuss how language can shape our understanding of a concept or category.

➢ Connecting Intertextual Themes, Reading Adinkra Symbols in Queen Pokou
This activity helps students understand the visual language of Adinkra symbols and their proverbial associations among Akan and Baoulé speakers. Interpreting the symbols provides insight into how polylingual and polyphonic elements create multiple layers of meaning in Tadjo's text.
Using the "Adinkra Symbols with Meanings" website, identify the symbols that open each chapter of *Queen Pokou*. Take time to read the descriptions and listen to the Akan pronunciations provided. Imagine the Adinkra symbols lined up along a strip of woven fabric. Consider their meanings in sequence and explain how you interpret this ensemble of symbols. Next, consider each Adinkra symbol in dialogue with the *Queen Pokou* chapter it introduces. How do the symbols inform our understanding of key themes? Explain your choices.

Engaging language policies and poetics 39

➢ Close Reading Activity, Orature and Styles in *Queen Pokou*
This is a follow-up activity to the Adinkra symbols activity. As students report on their observations, it is important to draw their attention to how polyphonic and polylingual elements are presented in both the French original and English translation of Tadjo's text.
When and how does Tadjo include elements from oral literary traditions (proverbs, folktales, songs, etc.) in her variations on the Queen Pokou tale? How are these songs and stories presented to readers? Pay attention to the linguistic interplay and textual arrangement of these resonant elements. What effect does this blending of oral and written literary styles create?

➢ Close Reading Activity, Focus on Languages and Styles in *Dog Days*
As a setup for this activity, students in small groups are assigned a passage from the text to analyze. Regardless of their level of linguistic expertise (or lack thereof), students work with both the French original and the English translation for this activity.
Identify passages in which Nganang infuses his work with the sonorities of multiple languages, dialects, and registers. Consider how nonstandard words are presented in the original and translated versions. Start by pinpointing utterances you would classify as translingual or nonstandard. Justify your choices. Next, pay attention to typographic and contextual cues. Are the words translated or defined for readers? If so, when and how? Is this pattern consistent when words are repeated throughout the text? What effect does this create? How do plurilingual aspects of the text reflect and reinforce important themes Nganang explores in his text?

➢ Language and Identity, Pragmatics and Social Cues in *The Wedding Party*
As a setup for this activity, students read Antonia Folarin Schleicher's article "Using Greetings to Teach Cultural Understanding" and complete a multimedia lesson on Yoruba greetings through the University of Georgia's African Studies Institute website.
As you watch *The Wedding Party*, pay attention to when characters speak in English and in Yoruba. Be particularly mindful of multilingual characters. Make a note of when they shift from one language to another. Do you detect any patterns or conventions to their choices? Justify your responses.
Beyond spoken language, pay attention to pragmatic cues. Imagine that you are a guest of Dunni's family. As you observe the interactions of the guests gathered to celebrate Dunni and Dozie's

wedding, who is doing their best to welcome and respect your family? Who is being linguistically or culturally insensitive? Explain your choices by interpreting different characters' verbal and nonverbal cues. How do linguistic and cultural cues inform your impressions and experience of the film?

Evaluation

This course combines summative and formative modes of assessment. In evaluating student performances and productions, assessments are designed to support student learning as process. In terms of formative measures, assessment activities guide students to identify and articulate their research topics; design and conduct their analysis, provide constructive feedback to peers, review and revise their projects-in-progress, and compose and communicate their findings in oral and written formats. These assignments, which culminate in a conference-length article, include an abstract development workshop, annotated bibliography, individual draft-in-progress conference, and poster presentation session.

Weekly homework and quiz activities help students hone their skills in interpreting literary and cinematic texts; making critical observations about thematic and formal patterns; and providing evidence from primary sources to support their ideas. The midterm exam features both written and oral components. In the writing section, students complete two tasks. They perform a close reading analysis of a single text and then compare the development of a key theme across two or more texts. For the oral exam, students set up individual meetings. They are assigned one question to prepare in advance such as "Identify a short passage from a text we have read that communicates a major theme in a compelling way. Come prepared to share your quote and explain your selection, highlighting the important form-meaning connections." The second part of the oral exam involves randomly selected short-answer questions designed to elicit paragraph-length responses. If students provide incomplete or incorrect information, the oral exam format creates opportunities to ask follow up questions and give immediate feedback on assessment items. It also creates time to check in with students individually and attend to their questions or concerns.

Student feedback

Both quantitative and qualitative student feedback have been overwhelmingly positive. Although the institutional course evaluations do not assess the translingual aspects of the course, when the course was last offered, 92%–100% of students reported being completely satisfied with all areas of curricular design, implementation, and instruction—including intellectual challenge, course assignments, classroom climate, and instructor support. Some of the key takeaways from the qualitative comments were a widespread appreciation for the multiliteracies objectives (including both the plurilingual and multimedia content and activities), and a prevailing sense of gratitude for the flexible structure and clear communication. This last point is particularly compelling given the translingual nature of the course. Moreover, many students expressed how the course changed the ways in which they perceive and experience their own identities as global citizens.

Caveats and reflections

Overall, this course is successful in promoting the objectives of multiliteracies pedagogies in a translingual classroom setting. Moreover, it provides ways to support heritage speakers and foreign language learners in programs where advanced-level language offerings are limited or nonexistent. Despite these positive outcomes, there are also challenges to implementing and administering this type of course. First and foremost, instructors must be familiar with how to conduct linguistic proficiency assessments or have access to support staff who can provide these diagnostic services. Then, once student proficiency levels have been determined, it may be necessary to adapt dual-language assignments and activities to match their individual skillsets and learning objectives. This requires extra time, organization, and availability on the part of the instructor. Another challenge involves acknowledging the impossibility of being (even novice-level) proficient in every language the class will encounter in this translingual classroom setting. Nevertheless, rather than view this situation as a limitation, it is imperative to recognize the opportunities it provides to connect with heritage speakers of languages like Akan and Yoruba who can serve as guest informants, either in person or with the help of digital and/or multimedia technologies. This support for plurilingual communities within and beyond the space of the classroom represents yet another way to impart the important and impactful objectives of both language learning and multiliteracies pedagogies.

References

Adichie, Chimamanda Ngozi. "The Danger of a Single Story." *TED Global*, July 2009, www.ted.com/talks/chimamanda_adichie_the_danger_of_a_single_story.

American Council on the Teaching of Foreign Languages. *Proficiency Guidelines*, 2012, www.actfl.org/sites/default/files/pdfs/public/ACTFLProficiencyGuidelines2012_FINAL.pdf.

Modern Language Association. "Foreign Languages and Higher Education: New Structures for a Changed World." *Profession* 2007, MLA, 2007, pp. 234–245.

The National Standards Collaborative Board. *World Readiness Standards for Learning Languages*. 4th ed., Author, 2015.

New London Group. "A Pedagogy of Multiliteracies: Designing Social Futures." *Harvard Educational Review*, vol. 66, no. 1, 1996, pp. 60–92.

Paesani, Kate et al. *A Multiliteracies Framework for Collegiate Foreign Language Teaching*. Pearson, 2015.

Warner, Chantelle, and Dupuy, Beatrice. "Moving toward Multiliteracies in Foreign Language Teaching: Past and Present Perspectives... and Beyond." *Foreign Language Annals*, vol. 51, no. 1, spring 2018, pp. 116–128.

Teaching material references

Abani, Chris. *The Face: Cartography of the Void*. Restless Books, 2016.

Adetiba, Kemi, director. *The Wedding Party*. FilmOne Distribution, 2016.

African Symbols and Proverbs. "Adinkra Symbols with Meanings." *Adinkra Symbols*, 2016, www.adinkrasymbols.org/.

Arimah, Lesley Nneka. *What It Means When a Man Falls from the Sky*. Riverhead Books, 2017.

Gyasi, Yaa. *Homegoing*. Knopf, 2016.

Meltzer, Jamie, director. *Welcome to Nollywood*. Outpost Studios, 2007.

Nganang, Patrice. *Temps de chien*. Serpent à Plumes, 2001.

———. *Dog Days*. Translated by Amy Baram Reid, University of Virginia Press, 2006.

Schleicher, Antonia Folarin. "Using Greetings to Teach Cultural Understanding." *The Modern Language Journal*, vol. 81, no. 3, autumn 1997, pp. 334–343.

Sissako, Abderrahmane, director. *Timbuktu*. Le Pacte, 2014.

Tadjo, Véronique. *Reine Pokou: Concerto pour un sacrifice*. Actes Sud, 2005.

———. *Queen Pokou: Concerto for a Sacrifice*. Translated by Amy Baram Reid, Ayebia Clarke Publishing, 2009.

University of Georgia African Studies Institute. "Kíkí Clcgb Cni" *Yoruba Classroom*, Unit 1, Lesson 1, www.africa.uga.edu/Yoruba/unit_01/lesson1.html.

4 Finding meaning in translation: critical reading for Japanese literature and film in translation

Chiaki Takagi

Course Title: JNS230 Women in Japanese Literature and Film
Course Level: Sophomore
Language(s) in Focus: Japanese
Course Type: Japanese Studies (literature and film), International and Global Studies (Asian Studies focus), Women's and Gender Studies

Contextualization of topic

Drawing examples from literature and film, the course examines Japanese society, with a special focus on its relationship to women's lives and women's roles from the Meiji period (1868–1912) to the present.

Course logistics

This 3-credit-hour course meets twice a week and each class session is 75 min. long. The instruction is delivered entirely face-to-face. The course carries the General Education Category Designation markers of Global Non-Western, Literature, and Speaking Intensive. The course also fulfills part of the degree requirements for the International and Global Studies major/minor and the Women's and Gender Studies major/minor.

Course objectives

The objective of the course is to enhance students' understanding of Japanese culture and society through close examination of the representation of women in Japanese literature and film. The teaching strategies behind the course aim to improve students' cross-cultural competency through intensive lectures, presentations, and discussion-oriented sessions.

Learning outcomes

Upon successful completion of this course, students will be able to demonstrate

- Reading skills required to read texts analytically and critically
- Effective oral communication skills through formal and informal speech
- Ability to discuss orally and in writing some of the important characteristics of Japanese literature from different time periods
- Ability to discuss (orally and in writing) gender issues in social and historical contexts by using various examples drawn from the writings and films
- Understanding of and sensitivity to cultural differences

Curricular structure

In designing the course, I took the backward design approach with clear goals of promoting critical reading of literature and film and enhancing students' global competency including awareness of linguistic differences.

Grade composition

(5%) Class Attendance: Students are expected to attend all class sessions.

(10%) Participation in Discussion/Class Activities: Students are expected to participate in class activities. This also includes being prepared for class, which reflects completion of reading/film viewing assignments. Preparation may be measured through unannounced writing or speaking prompts in class. Even if students are physically present, unless they participate in class activities, their participation points will be lowered.

(15%) Individual Speech: One formal oral presentation is required. Each student chooses a women/gender related topic that is inspired by a reading, film, and/or class discussion and orally discusses his/her ideas and thoughts on it, focusing on one (or two closely related) point(s) rather than discussing a whole text or film broadly. Students also submit a 2–3-page summary paper.

(25%) Book/Film Papers: Students are required to write three papers (two on books and one on a film) and in each paper they are expected to discuss the representation of women and gender issues in connection with the historical, societal and/or cultural background the book or film represents. The second book paper requires close reading of a paragraph or quote that they think represents the author's view of women. Papers are weighted equally.

(20%) Final Individual Speech: Students choose a book written by a Japanese author or a Japanese language film, which they would recommend for this course. Then they discuss why they think the book or film will help the students in this course to deepen their understanding of Japanese society in relation to women's lives.

(25%) Group Project: Each group will do research on an assigned topic. Students share research findings with the class and facilitate class discussion. Each group is expected to develop 3–4 discussion questions that are related to their assigned topic (examples below). Depending on the class size, the group size and topics may be adjusted.

Topics

- Poets and modern girls in the early modern period (Meiji 1868–1912, Taisho 1912–1926): female poets, *Bluestocking* and modern girls (moga)
- Women's lives during war time (1926–1945) and the early postwar period (post-Hiroshima/Nagasaki)
- Changing roles of women: family, marriage, gender roles, women in hyper-aged society
- Making changes: feminist movement/women's participation in politics/Lesbian, gay, bisexual, transgender, queer (LGBTQ) rights
- Media representation of female bodies (pop culture, *manga*, *anime*, idol culture, etc.) and Japan's sex industry
- Women's concerns (crimes involving women, sexual harassment, poverty, etc.)

Theoretical framework

The methodology of the course rests on a historical frame, and the course surveys women's positions in Japanese society chronologically (Ancient-Medieval, Edo, early modern period, postwar periods, and present). Lectures and reading/research assignments provide historical and social background. The course is also theme-based and students discuss various roles of women represented in literature and film. The course covers the following themes:

- Traditional roles of women
- Japan's modernization and women's roles
- Gender stereotypes and representation of Japanese women in media
- Changing roles of women/shifting of gender boundaries

The course assignments are divided into two categories: critical analysis of literature and film and guided research and presentations. The reading and writing assignments are designed to enhance students' close reading skills with the goal of improving their critical thinking skills. The research assignment provides cultural information that is necessary for understanding the literary works and film. The course assignments will enable students to identify and/or describe some of the various social, historical, cultural, and/or theoretical contexts in which literary texts have been written and interpreted. In order to bring authenticity to the materials and emphasize the importance of knowing the language, I use discussion topics that require critical reading based on comparisons between the original text and its English translation.

Teaching materials

The reading selections include literary texts, films, and other materials.

Readings

- "One Year Later," Hayashi, Mariko, translated by Giles Murray, 2004
- *Kafka on the Shore*, Murakami, Haruki, translated by Philip Gabriel, 2008
- *Naomi*, Tanizaki, Junichiro, translated by Anthony H. Chambers, 2001
- *Building Waves*, Tomioka, Taeko, translated by Louise Heal Kawai, 2012

Films

- *Black Rain*, Shohei Imamura, 1989
- *Caterpillar*, Wakamatsu, 2010
- *Fall Guy*, Kinji Fukasaku, 1982
- *Like Father, Like Son*, Hirokazu Koreeda, 2013
- *Tony Takitani*, Jun Ichikawa, 2005

Class activities

I prepare a PowerPoint presentation for each class session and spend roughly the first 30 min. presenting information. In my PowerPoint slides, I include a list of key terms and discussion questions from assigned readings and/or a film. Students share their ideas first in small groups (10 min.) and then the whole class has discussions (25 min.). I use the last 10 min. to sum up the discussion and draw conclusions.

➢ The First-Day Activity
On the first day of the class, I tell them that I would begin each class session with greetings in Japanese and teach greetings and basic phrases in Japanese (こんにちは。お元気ですか。はい、元気です。/ Hello. How are you? I am fine.). I also ask students to address me as 先生 (sensei = teacher) or Takagi sensei (I emphasize the word order as an English-Japanese difference).

➢ Background of Japanese Writing Systems
I schedule a Japanese history lesson that briefly covers all the time periods from the Jomon period to present day. As part of Japan's history, I introduce the history of Japanese writing (arrival of the *kanji* characters from China and development of the *kana* characters during the Heian period). I also show pictures of ancient writing (such as *Kojiki*) and *kana* writing (*The Tale of Genji*), and let students visually compare them with modern Japanese writing. Then, I discuss how the modern Japanese writing system works using a combination of *kanji* and *kana* scripts. I especially emphasize that *katakana* is used for foreign loan words. Some examples are *konpyūtaa* (computer), *nōsu karoraina* (North Carolina), and *aisukuriimu* (ice cream).

➢ Japanese Personal Names
In relation to the writing system, I discuss the significance of the personal names of the characters. In the film *Tony Takitani*, there is a Japanese character whose name is Tony Takitani. I point out that his name is unusual because of its order of the first and last names and because of its possible spelling, which implies the character's cultural hybridity. His name is written with half *katakana* and half *kanji* in the original literary work of Haruki Murakami. I also touch upon the Japanese names and correct pronunciation of the names of Japanese characters, such as that *ko* ending three syllabus names are usually for female, and that the /r/ in Tony's wife's name, Eriko should not be pronounced as /r/ as in English.

In Junichiro Tanizaki's *Naomi*, the narrator states that the main character's name, Naomi, is written with three *kanji* characters. I let students know that "Naomi" is a common Japanese female name, and I show the *kanji* spelling of the name. We then discuss the difference in the pronunciation between Naomi in Japanese and Naomi in English. I also point out that in the original Japanese text, the name is written with *katakana* because, according to the narrator, that is the best way to reflect the character's Western appearance, although this line of the narrator is left out in the English translation.

➢ Translation of the Titles

The relevance of translated titles of the literary works and films makes a great topic for the introduction of the original Japanese words. Usually a little linguistic explanation will allow students to compare the translated titles with the original. The original Japanese title of Junichiro Tanizaki's *Naomi* is *Chijin no Ai*. I explain each word (*chijin*=fool, *ai*=love) and ask whether the English title is an appropriate translation. The focal point of the Japanese title is the narrator, while that of the English title is Naomi.

We also discuss the significance of the use of *katakana* in the title of the film キャタピラー (*Kyatapira*/Caterpillar). This film is about the wife of a Japanese soldier who was sent back home without limbs. Its *katakana* title may be interpreted in a couple of ways: as a physically disabled husband and a freedom-less wife who wants to fly away; or as a tank caterpillar that symbolizes destructions of war, including Japanese soldiers' rapes and murders of Chinese victims. By using a *katakana* title, the film director may have attempted to avoid direct reference to the characters' physical appearance. It may also represent the filmmaker's intention to present war as a universal issue.

➢ Listening Exercises

Students watch the assigned films in Japanese with English subtitles. I ask them to pay special attention to how characters address each other in addition to the words they may hear repeatedly. For example, in *Caterpillar*, the wife addresses the husband as *Kyuzo-san* although the English translation shows it as *Kyuzo*. I point out that the use of suffix -*san* reflects the gender power dynamics.

Like Father, Like Son, is a story about two families whose sons were intentionally switched by a hospital nurse. The main character addresses himself as *papa* when he talks to his nonbiological son whom he raised, while he uses *otōsan* when he speaks to his biological son.

➢ Japanese English from the 1980s
As part of the 1980s women's culture, I introduce the trendy words of that time such as ボディコン (*bodikon*=body conscious) and ワンレン (*wanren*=one length hair) and have students think of the meanings of these "Japanese English" words. An examination of these words reveals how young women's culture was controlled by the media's dissemination of "fashionable" *katakana* words.

➢ Trendy Word Now and Then
When the class discusses "One Year Later," I let students guess the meaning of the popular word from the 1980s, 三高 (*Sanko*=3 high/a desirable man who is tall, highly educated and with high income) and ask them to draw examples of how this idea is reflected in the text. I also introduce the recent idea of women being *Sanko* (highly educated, high status, and high income).

Ideas for future class activities

For each reading, a new target Japanese word/expression may be introduced (e.g., *kawaii*). *Kawaii* is a relatively well-known Japanese word. The class will discuss the idea of *kawaii*. Then I will ask students if they think the word was used in any part of the novel, *Building Waves*, assuming they will recall the part in which the protagonist's face was described as "cute" by her younger lover. I will let them know that in the Japanese original text, *kawaii* is spelled with *katakana* when the female protagonist uses it, while it is written with *hiragana* when it is used by her lover. This observation could make an effective critical thinking question.

Evaluation

The course uses both formative assessments (class participation, speech, book/film papers) and summative assessments (group project and final speech, which includes a summary paper). Elements of the evaluation criteria for the final speech are included here.

Final speech

- Topic: Appropriate focus/coherence
- Content: Organization, clarity of ideas and thoughts, effective argument (supported by appropriate examples from literature and film)
- Delivery: Effective eye contact, timeliness, appropriateness of visual aids, clear voice
- Summary of Paper: Coherence, organization, clarity, grammar

Student feedback

In response to the statement "The course promoted cross-cultural understanding and/or awareness," 100% of nine responders marked 4 and above (out of 1–5 scale) in year 1, 88.9% (9 responders) in year 2, and 72.7% (12 responders) in year 3. Approximately 30% of the total of 74 students who completed the course in these years are those who have taken language courses and/or are currently taking Japanese with me. One of the students' comments reads, "JNS230 increased my motivation to study the language. I have always felt that reading or watching translations does not give you the full meaning or nuance behind what you are taking in. I wanted to have the ability to understand the meanings I was missing due to a language barrier." Another student wrote, "Every time we discussed a literary text I found it necessary to find the original Japanese name (title) so that I could further my understanding of the cultural significance of the text."

Caveats and reflections

The strength of this course is that language use plays a key role in several literary analysis and critical thinking exercises. The ways I introduced linguistic differences and meanings that are lost in translation enable students with little to no knowledge of the language to understand nuances and subtleties in the original works, which would otherwise be inaccessible to them. Students showed interest in linguistic differences, and they had thought-provoking discussions on topics related to translation. The course emphasizes the importance of reading literary works in their original language. However, it is also necessary to let students know that their ideas and thoughts based on their close readings, even in English translation, are valued and respected.

Offering attractive literature and cultural studies courses is a great strategy for recruiting more students into the study of foreign languages and maintaining higher retention rates. With a clear goal of promoting Japanese courses, surveys should have been conducted at the beginning to know how students feel about studying Japanese, and at the end of the course, to ask if this course has motivated them to pursue that academic pathway.

References

Murakami, Haruki 村上春樹. "Tony Takitani" トニー滝谷 [Tony Takitani] *Rekishinton no Yurei* レキシントンの幽霊 [The Ghost of Lexington] by Haruki Murakami, Bunshun Bunko, 2010, pp. 113–145.

Tanizaki, Junichiro 谷崎潤一郎. *Chijin no Ai*, 痴人の愛 [A Fool's Love]. Shincho Bunko, 2003.

Teaching material references

Black Rain. Directed by Shohei Imamura 今村昌平. 1989. AnimEigo, 2009. DVD.
Caterpillar. Directed by Koji Wakamatsu 若松考二. 2010. Lorber Films, 2012. DVD.
Fall Guy. Directed by Kinji Fuaksaku 深作欣司. 1982. Homevision, 2005. DVD.
Hayashi, Mariko. "One Year Later." Translated by Giles Murray, *Tokyo Fragments*, IBC Publishing, 2004, pp. 91–119.
Like Father, Like Son. Directed by Hirokazu Koreeda 是枝弘和. 2013. MPI Home Video, 2014. DVD.
Murakami, Haruki. *Kafka on the Shore*. Translated by Philip Gabriel, Vintage, 2008.
Tanizaki, Junichiro. *Naomi*. Translated by Anthony H. Chambers, Vintage International, 2001.
Tomioka, Taeko. *Building Waves*. Translated by Louise Heal Kawai, Dalkey Archive Press, 2012.
Tony Takitani. Directed by Jun Ichikawa 市川準. 2005. Strand Releasing Home Video, 2005. DVD.

5 Spanish Golden Age literature in the general education curriculum: sharing the riches of culture and language

Charlene Kalinoski

Course Title: INQ 271 The Golden Age of Spain: From Glory to Decadence
Course Level: Sophomore
Language(s) in Focus: Spanish
Course Type: This course is part of the college's General Education program, the Intellectual Inquiry (INQ) curriculum, which is taught by humanities faculty

Contextualization of topic

In my course offering, we explore the Spanish experience from the reign of Fernando and Isabel to the death of Carlos II through literary texts, historical essays, works of art, and a recent film set in the 17th century. The literary works consist of plays, novels, and poetry, and serve as the central nexus of the course.

Course logistics

This is a 4-credit-hour course that meets three times a week for 60 min. each session. As a General Education course taught in English, it is not intended to count toward the Spanish major or minor. However, because we allow students to take a maximum of two discipline-related courses taught in English toward the Spanish major, we have counted it for the major in a limited number of cases. There are no prerequisites for the course.

Course objectives

The course objectives are to be stated in an "inquiry" format that consists of questions addressed during the course.

Spain's immense political power in the 16th and 17th centuries was accompanied by impressive cultural developments in literature and the arts and is known as its Golden Age. We will approach this period through the following questions:

- How did Spain develop from a group of medieval kingdoms to a nation and then an empire?
- Why was the Spanish empire an "improbable" one and what led to its decline?
- What is the Black Legend and how did it affect perceptions about Spain over the centuries?
- What are some of the great literary works of that era that have endured to our time?
- What is narrative theory and how can it help us to analyze narratives of any genre or period?
- Which works of art capture the essence of the age?
- How has this period been interpreted and presented in a recent film set in 17th-century Spain?

Learning outcomes

There are standardized learning outcomes for all sections of INQ 271. Students will be able to

- Apply humanities methodologies appropriate for the course's discipline and topic
- Write about course topics clearly and effectively
- Communicate effectively about the course topic in an oral format

Curricular structure

We engage in close readings of texts to promote critical thinking and to understand works created in historical and social conditions very different from our own, as we search for commonalities and points of contact.

The final grade is based on the following components:

(38%) Midterm and Final Exams
(38%) Two textual commentaries 5–6 pages in length
(10%) Oral presentation on an historical or cultural topic
(10%) Quizzes at the beginning of most classes on the assigned readings
(4%) Discussion Leader once during the semester

The textual commentaries and oral presentation are evaluated via rubrics that are used throughout the Intellectual Inquiry curriculum. Having common rubrics keeps instructors from every department on track and, most importantly, assists student learning and follows individual student progress over time.

Theoretical framework

INQ 271 courses are inquiry-based and require instructors to introduce methodologies of the humanities and allow students to practice their application. We address the essential questions posed in the course objectives through the texts and other materials we cover for which I provide essential context including Spanish language content. I incorporate narrative theory to serve as the humanities methodology which we explore through H. Porter Abbott's *The Cambridge Introduction to Narrative*. This text enables students to see beyond the "story" of a literary work or film to understanding it as narrative discourse, a complex network of rhetorical elements.

Teaching materials

Required texts

- *Don Quijote*, Miguel de Cervantes, translated by Burton Raffel, 1999
- *Life Is a Dream and Other Spanish Classics*, edited by Eric Bentley, 2004
- *The Cambridge Introduction to Narrative*, H. Porter Abbott, 2008
- *The Dog in the Manger*, Lope de Vega, translated by David Johnson, 2004
- *The Life of Lazarillo de Tormes*, Anonymous, translated by W.S. Merwin, 2005

Additional teaching materials may be found in the References section.

Class activities

Sample plan for a 60-min. class focused on reviewing one act of a play and material in the *Cambridge Introduction to Narrative*.

- (5–7 min.) Brief quiz to check completion of assigned reading.
- (5–8 min.) Student discussion leader's presentation on assigned reading.

Spanish Golden Age literature 55

- (15 min.) Class discussion of assigned text. I answer questions and insert contextual material. We review character names and place names, pronouncing them in Spanish and locating the latter on maps and through other visual material.
- (15 min.) Act it out! I divide students into groups to read through selected passages which they perform for the rest of class as time allows.
- (15 min.) Review of assigned reading in *The Cambridge Introduction to Narrative* with class discussion aimed at making connections with the literary text being studied.

Concrete examples of class activities centered on Spanish-language content:

➢ Exploration of the meaning of the title of the play *Fuenteovejuna*
Early in our reading of this work, we practice saying the name in Spanish and discuss what it means. What initially looks like a long and curious foreign word has two parts, *fuente* "drinking fountain" and *ovejuna* "an adjective related to sheep." The title is sometimes translated as "the sheep's well." I then tell them to keep the meaning of title in mind as we progress through the work. Is it merely the name of the village where much of the action occurs or does it have a deeper meaning? Do any of the characters comment on the name *Fuenteovejuna* during the play? Why and in what context? This activity in intended to promote a close reading in keeping with the spirit of "inquiry." It sets the stage for a longer discussion when we reach the end of the work. Why did Lope de Vega choose to name this play *Fuenteovejuna* instead of another title? What could have been some alternates? Why does the title *Fuenteovejuna* especially suit the work? This exercise is repeated for the titles of the other works we read and for the film, *Alatriste*. Do the original titles in Spanish tell us something that the English titles do not? Are there significant differences between the two?
➢ Reading Sor Juana Inés de la Cruz's poetry in English and in Spanish
During our study of Sor Juana, I read the sonnets we are covering in Spanish so students can hear the original rhymes. I display the Spanish and English versions side by side and ask students to look for cognates or words they recognize from previous study of Spanish as applicable. (The well-known sonnet that begins "World, in hounding me, what do you gain?/*En perseguirme, mundo, ¿qué interesas?*" works very well as do others.)
➢ Review of webpage that presents a typical Spanish Golden Age theatre, a *corral de comedias*, and its parts

Because the web material is presented in Spanish, I review the parts of the theater in Spanish with translations and explanations in English. Each student creates their own drawing as we go over the different areas of the *corral*, labeling its parts in English and Spanish. When they are tested on this material, I provide them with a sketch of a *corral* and ask them to label and explain it. If they provide the names of the parts of the theater in Spanish in addition to English, they get extra credit. Some students tell me they prefer the Spanish terms to their English counterparts. For them, the word *mosqueteros* is more memorable than "groundlings."

➢ Making Spanish pronunciation matter
Since an oral presentation is one of the course requirements and the rubric for the assignment measures "fluent delivery and correct pronunciation," being able to pronounce the names of historical or cultural figures and locations adequately in Spanish is an appropriate expectation. I offer to work with students individually as needed. In our globalized world, learning to pronounce key foreign words is important, a point I emphasize throughout the semester.

Ideas for future class activities

- I plan to add a stronger art component to the course. To this end, I will provide a list of iconic works of art for students to investigate in groups of two that they will present to the class in brief (5 min.) presentations. The titles of the works will be presented in English and Spanish to address the question: by what names are the works known in the Spanish-speaking world? To make this project more sharable, we will upload each group's material to a WordPress site or some other appropriate digital platform.
- Another idea is to create a digital humanities project in the form of a timeline onto which we will add the historical, literary, and cultural material we cover during the semester. The names of historical figures and events, literary works and their authors, etc. will be provided in English and Spanish, giving it more of a bilingual character. This class project will be completed by the end of the semester to serve as part of a general review.

Evaluation

The course implements both formative (quizzes, class discussions), and summative assessments (midterm, final exam, oral presentation and textual commentaries). All INQ 271 courses are required to include 10–15 pages of formal writing and one oral presentation. I evaluate their textual commentaries and oral presentations based on the following:

Textual commentaries evaluation

- Focus and thesis: Focused thesis reflects complexity and nuanced understanding of topic
- Reasoning: Demonstrates sophistication of thought, recognizing multiple dimensions and/or perspectives as appropriate
- Evidence: Relevant, accurate, well-integrated, and well-documented
- Organization: Rationale, sensible, and deliberate structure that enhances and clarifies meaning
- Style and mechanics: Effective sentence structure that is rich, well-chosen, reflecting a variety of sentence styles and length, and free of grammatical errors

Oral presentation evaluation

Content

- Purpose and Focus: Central idea is clear and reflects purpose
- Organization and Development: Clear, logical, and deliberate
- Content and Supporting Material: Material is interesting, relevant, accurate, and well-documented
- Visual Aids (if required): Promotes communication and adds value

Delivery

- Eye Contact: Consistent eye contact with entire audience, speaker seldom refers to notes
- Mannerisms: Actively support and aid message
- Verbal Skills: Delivered with fluency and energy

Caveats and reflections

Teaching the Spanish Golden Age and sharing Spanish culture and language in a General Education course is beneficial for students and foreign language departments. When my institution adopted a new General Education curriculum almost ten years ago, the language requirement was strengthened to include three semesters of study. This meant that lower-level language courses would be taught mainly by nontenure track full-time faculty and adjuncts, so that tenured faculty could teach courses like the one described here. In all honesty, the first iteration of this course was an uncomfortable experience for me, mainly because I was teaching a Spanish topic in English and had to retool my pedagogy for students who were not in my class primarily to learn language. It was rewarding, however, to share material I love with a broader range of students. Besides, which other faculty member at my college would teach this course if I did not? The Intellectual Inquiry courses have taken my colleagues and me out of our departmental silo. Some students have found a path to the Spanish major and minor programs through my course, particularly in its more recent iterations. My last two offerings of The Golden Age of Spain yielded four Spanish majors or minors, drawing students to our language program that we otherwise might have lost.

As for caveats associated with teaching the course, there are a few. Some students have come to my class expecting a history course rather than one with a strong literary and cultural vein. Therefore, I explain that history's role in the course, while important, is not dominant. Second, it is necessary to rethink one's pedagogy. Teaching chapters from *Don Quijote* in English does not require comprehension checks or focusing on providing comprehensible input, but may necessitate developing appropriate methods for students learning the material in their native language. And third, it is necessary to remember one's audience. Students will not be as comfortable with Spanish words and names as are our majors and minors; they will need patient assistance over the course of the semester along with reminders about why making the effort to pronounce foreign words correctly matters. Ultimately, my students leave the class with some Spanish pronunciation skills and a more global perspective, one that is derived from the course content as well as from stepping over the borders of language.

Reference

Johnson, Steven. "A College Lost Its Languages One by One. Can 3 Professors Save Spanish?" *Chronicle of Higher Education*, 8 February 2019.

Teaching material references

Abbott, H. Porter. *The Cambridge Introduction to Narrative*. 2nd ed., Cambridge University Press, 2008.

Alatriste. Directed by Agustín Díaz Yanes, 20th Century Fox, 2006.

Bentley, Eric, editor. *Life Is a Dream and Other Spanish Classics*. Translated by Roy Campbell, Applause, 2004.

Cervantes, Miguel de. *Don Quijote*. Translated by Burton Raffel, W.W. Norton, 1999.

Spanish Golden Age literature 59

Conquistadors. Directed by David Wallace, PBS Home Video, 2001.
El perro del hortelano. Directed by Miró, Pilar, Tribanda Pictures, 1996.
Kamen, Henry. "Vicissitudes of a World Power." *Spain. A History*. Edited by Raymond Carr, Oxford University Press, 2000, pp. 152–172.
The Life of Lazarillo de Tormes. Translated by W.S. Merwin, New York Review Books, 2005.
"The Myth of the Spanish Inquisition." *Timewatch*, Season 13, Episode 7. BBC/A&E Video, 1994, YouTube.
Tabuenca, Elia. "Partes de un corral de comedias." UnPROFESOR, 15 Nov. 2018. www.unprofesor.com/lengua-espanola/partes-de-un-corral-de-comedias-1537.html.
Trueblood, Alan S., trans. *A Sor Juana Anthology*. Harvard University Press, 1988.
Vega, Lope de. *The Dog in the Manger*. Translated by David Johnson, Oberon Books, 2004.

Part II
Linguistics

6 Japanese and English in contact: linguistic and cultural perspectives

Priya Ananth

Course Title: HUM 3000 Topics in Foreign Language Linguistics
Course Level: Upper-Division
Language(s) in Focus: Japanese
Course Type: Humanities, Sociolinguistics

Contextualization of topic

This course coalesces around the language contact phenomenon, an important and well-researched field of study in the discipline of sociolinguistics (Heine and Kuteva). "Language Contact" refers to the linguistic interaction between two or more languages that often leads to the languages evolving because of the impact they receive from each other at the lexical as well as at the grammatical level (Thomason and Kaufman). In the case of Japanese and English interaction specifically, almost 10% of modern colloquial Japanese uses English in some form such as loanwords, borrowings, or English words created in Japan (Stanlaw, Loveday). *The Iwanami Dictionary* records that of all the foreign words that appear therein, almost 80% are of English origin. The Japanese language, throughout its history, has been strongly influenced linguistically by other foreign languages, and especially, English. This course focuses on the language contact phenomenon between English and Japanese, taking into consideration linguistic and cultural perspectives associated with this phenomenon. Inclusion of the cultural perspectives is justified in two ways. First, evolution and devolution of language do not happen in vacuum. They are, in most cases, accompanied by historical, political, or cultural motivations and outcomes. Second, broadening the scope of the course was an initial step toward the planning of a curriculum that could attract a broader audience.

Course logistics

Designed for face-to-face teaching on campus, this 3-credit-hour course meets twice weekly for 85 min. For students minoring in Linguistics Studies or Humanities, this course counts as an upper-division core elective. There are no language prerequisites for this course.

Course objectives

There are four main goals identified and listed on the syllabus:

- To understand the language contact process from a linguistic perspective
- To understand and analyze the use of English language in modern Japan and be able to apply the language contact mechanisms to the particular case of Japanese English
- To critically examine the principles and mechanisms in a wide variety of contemporary genres and be able to apply them to other foreign languages
- To appreciate the fact that in this world of globalization, linguistic imperialism no longer exists in any country

Learning outcomes

The course objectives are tied to the following learning outcomes:

- Upon completion of the course, students will be able to understand the language contact process as a sociolinguistic phenomenon and will be able to interpret its manifestations in not just Japanese and English, but also in other foreign languages.
- By way of examining and analyzing the various linguistic and cultural mechanisms of language contact in the particular case of Japanese English, students will be able to develop critical thinking skills that they will be able to then apply to other foreign languages or area studies.
- Through class discussions, writing assignments, and oral presentations, students will be able to communicate their research findings and opinions to their peers.
- Students will be able to read and write *katakana* and *hiragana*, and will be able to interpret the linguistics concepts learned in this course using examples in Japanese at the lexical and phrasal levels.

Curricular structure

This course was constructed using the backward design approach (Wiggins and McTighe) that places learning outcomes and assessment procedures at the center of the course planning process. In other words, this approach strategically puts focus on the questions and tasks that provide evidence of learning, rather than focusing solely on covering the content from the syllabus. Following this approach, evaluation criteria were put in place before deciding on the theoretical framework, course content, and class activities.

Grade composition

(20%) Attendance and Class Participation
(20%) Unit Exams
(20%) Mini Class Presentations
(20%) Weekly Reflection Questions
(20%) Final Project

Class Participation is evaluated based on active participation in class discussions and in question/answer sessions.

Unit Exams measure the content knowledge that the students have acquired and retained in specific units. There are three unit exams during the semester.

Mini Class Presentations are student-led, short class presentations followed by discussions based on the reading materials assigned for the day. Each student is responsible for making two presentations during the course.

Weekly Reflection Questions are created by the students and turned in once a week. These questions are collected and used for class discussions held at the end of each class period and on test review days.

Final Projects consist of a final research paper and a class presentation on the language contact phenomenon as seen in languages other than English. The students may select any foreign language and research the manifestations of English (and/or other languages) within the linguistic, social, cognitive, or cultural spheres of the countries in which these languages are used. An important requirement of the final project is to demonstrate the phenomenon through the actual use of the language.

Theoretical framework

As I was following a backward design approach to build the curriculum, it was inevitable that I consider the final project requirements first, before going any further. Since the final project requires students to examine the manifestations of English (and/or other foreign languages) within the linguistic, social, cognitive, or cultural spheres of another language, it is imperative to present an example of these requirements in the specific case of Japanese and English. Also, inclusion of the actual language to demonstrate language contact phenomenon is the other important requirement of student projects. This creates the need to incorporate elementary-level Japanese language into the curriculum as well. Based on the two main parameters that emerge from the requirements of the final project (stay relevant to the theme, and incorporate the actual foreign language), I decided to select a thematic unit or theme-based approach as the pedagogical framework for this course. This approach is one where the main topic is divided into a series of stand-alone modules or units that are interrelated to each other by a recurring theme. Tohsaku defines a thematic unit as "an instructional unit that organizes teaching around themes or topics, and makes it possible for us to integrate instruction across such areas as language, culture, science, art, literature, social issues" (handout). For this course, there are nine thematic units:

- Theories and Mechanisms of the Language Contact Process
- Dynamics of the Japanese Language
- History of Language Contact in Japan
- Language Contact in J-pop Verses and Poetics
- Language Contact in Japanese Foods
- Language Contact in Advertising (Print Media) and TV Commercials
- Language Contact in Color Nomenclature
- Language Contact in Second Language Acquisition
- Japanese Attitudes toward Language Contact

While these modules or thematic units are stand-alone themes, they are all weaved into the main topic on the phenomenon of language contact. The first unit on theories, mechanics, and general background, as well as the second unit on the structure of the Japanese language, lay the foundation for the remaining seven units. I devote about three weeks on the first two units and focus on introducing the Japanese syllabaries, writing system, and selected lexicons to novice learners of Japanese.

Teaching materials

There is one required textbook for this course, in combination with a list of supplemental required readings.

- *Japanese English: Language and Culture Contact*, James Stanlaw, 2004

For additional selected readings, see the References section.

Japanese and English in contact 67

Class activities

The class employs a lecture and discussion format. Class activities include lectures, student presentations, and group and pair discussions based on reflection questions prepared by the students. Here is an example of a typical lesson plan for an 85-min. class:

- (20 min.) Mini student presentation on assigned reading material
- (10 min.) Q/A and discussions on student presentation
- (45 min.) Lecture
- (10 min.) Pair and group work based on reflection questions

Specific examples and accompanying sample questions of material used for the module on "Language Contact in Advertising" are as follows:

➢ My Switch

Figure 6.1 My Switch 1.
Photo Provided by Priya Ananth.

Figure 6.2 My Switch 2.
Photo Provided by Priya Ananth.

- What do you think is depicted in these images?
- Extract keywords that appear in English, in Japanese, and in Japanized English. Discuss the impact of using English/Japanized English on the marketability of this product. Think from the point of view of a consumer.
- Compare the use of "my" in "My Switch" and "watashi no" (mine). Compare the usage of "my" in other occurrences such as "my coffee," "my car," and "my home."

➢ Resortful

Figure 6.3 Resortful.
Photo Provided by Priya Ananth.

- Comment on the image of what seems like a poster for inviting visitors to Hawaii.
- What do you think "resortful" means in this context?
- This is a Japanized English word coined for a Japanese audience. Do you think the word would serve as an effective strategy to draw visitors to Hawaii?

70 *Priya Ananth*

➢ Eki na Cafe

Figure 6.4 Eki na Cafe.
Photo Provided by Priya Ananth.

- This was a picture taken at a train station in front of a coffee shop. The words *eki* (station) and café are connected in a way that *eki* (station) is modifying café like an adjective. How would you translate the name of this café for someone who can read English, but does not understand what is written here?
- The unconventional usage of *eki* (station) as an adjective is not grammatical in the Japanese language. What do you think is the motivation for this atypical language structure?
- If you were to create a newly coined Japanized English expression to describe a pizza place, what would that be? Use words in Japanese or any other language that do not necessarily carry their original meaning. You can give them your own meaning and interpretation.

Japanese and English in contact 71

➢ Sunao

Figure 6.5 Sunao.
Photo Provided by Priya Ananth.

- *Sunao* in Japanese literally means the state of being gentle and obedient often associated with good daughters who follow the advice of their elders without questioning. What is the significance of using this term in this billboard for ice cream and cookies?
- Why is only *sunao* written in Romanization, while the others are not? What might be the reason for this choice of orthography?
- Can you identify one original Japanese word that is written in *katakana* syllabary? Give reasons why *katakana* was the syllabary of choice for this word?

72 *Priya Ananth*

➢ Tomodachi Burger

Figure 6.6 Tomodachi Burger.
Photo Provided by Tomodachi Initiative, US-Japan Council.

- In 2013, Wendy's in Japan released an ad seeking ideas for the creation of a new recipe for a "Tomodachi Burger" meaning "friend burger." Comment on the writing style used for naming this new burger.
- What is the significance of using Romanization for Japanese words, such as *tomodachi*? What is the global message implied by this choice of writing style?
- The character depicting Wendy in the ad is not the original American Wendy, but a Japanized version of her. What subtle impact do you see in the use of a Japanese character for an American fast food company?

Time permitting, lecture is followed by pair and group discussions based on reflection questions submitted by students. Here are some examples of reflection questions:

- Why might English-inspired vocabulary or *wasei eigo* be a better term for English loanwords in Japanese than "borrowings"?
- According to traditional (pre-World War II) Japanese morality, why is the loanword *mai* (my) controversial and considered selfish?
- Why is the word "diet" less favorable than the word "light" when referring to foods and drinks that are lower in calories and/or sugar in Japan?
- Why is English used to express Japanese domestic life? Would Japanese not be the more suitable form of expression?
- Japanese advertisements and television commercials tend to play on emotions with great success. In America, when advertisements or commercials play to an audience's emotions, it seems less effective. Why is this? What could Japanese advertising agencies teach American agencies about playing on emotions?

Ideas for future class activities

- Since study abroad programs offer a dynamic platform to observe and experience language contact in action, this course could be adapted to a study abroad curriculum. Some activities could include taking pictures of various instances of language contact, and creating a photo diary, or surveying Japanese people and coming up with lists of words or phrases they frequently use in English. Data could be analyzed based on age group, gender, etc.
- An activity similar to the one described above could be included locally on campus with visiting foreign exchange students or foreign residents in the community.
- Interactive quizzes based on game formats could be included to test linguistic concepts as well as language basics as part of the formative assessments.

Evaluation

I employed both formative and summative forms of assessment. Through mini presentations, class participation, unit tests, and reflection questions, I measured the daily and weekly progress of students.

These formative assessment tools assisted me in periodically gauging the amount of material learned by the students. The final project was a summative assessment used to determine if the students could apply what they had learned from Japanese to a different foreign language and construct opinions and perspectives based on facts, mechanisms, and background research. They had the freedom to select languages of their choice as long as they were within the realm of the language contact phenomenon. Another important requirement was to incorporate examples using original orthography in that language. This encouraged the students to look at the language contact phenomenon as an organic and dynamic process between different languages. Here is a sample of final project topics:

- *La questionne della lingua*: Are English loanwords de-beautifying Italian?
- The history of Gaelic and unexpected loanwords in English
- No "Z" in Brazil: Phonotactic and lexical borrowing in Brazil's international communities
- English in Filipino advertising
- Arabic loanwords in Spanish: History of contact and phonetic assimilation

Student feedback

The standard course evaluation questionnaire used by my institution yielded the following responses specific to foreign language use:

- Motivated to sign up for the Japanese language course next semester
- Course helped understand Japanese language better
- NHK online resource (radio and TV broadcast) introduced in this class will be a great resource as I continue to study Japanese on my own after graduation
- Took this course prior to doing a study abroad in Japan. Felt better prepared

Caveats and reflections

The course proved beneficial for student recruitment and retention. It motivated novice students to start learning Japanese and continuing students to stay invested by deepening their knowledge of the language. Moreover, the course raised students' awareness and understanding of the relationship between Japanese language and sociolinguistic phenomena, which makes language learning more meaningful and provides a further rationale for students to study Japanese. In order to attract a broad cross-section of students, the instructor must be ready to invest a good amount of time explaining the concept of this interdisciplinary course and educating students about its potential benefits. Among these benefits is the ability to refine critical thinking skills by delving deep into linguistics topics, allowing students to develop both a keen awareness and a profound understanding of connections of foreign languages to other areas of study. In this way, the course lends itself to cross-listing with related areas such as linguistics, English, and education. With some creativity, the course content and format can be easily adapted to other foreign languages. The benefits of a course such as this one are not for students alone. As a professor, making the connection between humanities content and language, is refreshing and rewarding because it allows me to look at both of them in a new way that fosters my own critical thinking, creativity, and professional development.

References

Heine, Bernd, and Tania Kuteva. *Language Contact and Grammatical Change.* Cambridge University Press, 2005.
Iwanami Japanese Dictionary. 1960. Iwanami, 2001.
Loveday, Leo. *Language Contact in Japan.* Oxford University Press, 1996.
Thomason, Sara, and Terrence Kaufman. *Language Contact, Creolization, and Genetic Linguistics.* University of California Press, 1989.
Tohsaku, Yasuhiko. *AATJ Language Culture and Technology Institute in Japan.* Handout, 2010.
Wiggins, Grant, and Jay McTighe. *Understanding by Design.* Pearson Education, 2005.

Teaching material references

Abe, Keiko. "Japanese Attitudes Towards Foreign Languages." *Collegium Antropologicum*, vol. 28, supplement 1, 2004, pp. 115–122.
Browne, Kevin C., and Richard Lee. "Context and Contact: the Impact of a Japanese International University Environment on Japanese Use outside the Classroom." *Polyglossia*, vol. 20, 2011, pp. 5–13.
Daulton, Frank. "English Learners' Attitudes Towards Gairaigo." *The Ryukoku Journal of Humanities and Sciences*, vol. 32, no. 2, 2011, pp. 1–11.
Holmquist, John P., and Andrew Cudmore. "English in Japanese and Philippine Advertising: An Exploratory Comparison." *The Journal of Global Business Management*, vol. 9, no. 1, 2013, pp. 82–91.

Inagawa, Mayuko. "Creative and Innovative Uses of English in Contemporary Japan." *English Today*, vol. 31, 2015, pp. 11–16.
Mckenzie, Robert M. "The Complex and Rapidly Changing Sociolinguistic Position of the English Language in Japan: A Summary of English Language Contact and Use." *Japan Forum*, vol. 20, no. 2, 2008, pp. 267–286.
Nyman, Kaisan. "English Influence on Japanese Popular Music: A Case Study of Language Contact." *Master's Thesis*, University of Eastern Finland, 2012.
Stanlaw, James. *Japanese English: Language and Culture Contact*. Hong Kong University Press, 2004.

7 Understanding key sociocultural concepts in Japanese: unlocking the door to communication

Kathy Negrelli

Course Title: ASIA 4490 Japanese Culture and Society
Course Level: Upper-Division
Language(s) in Focus: Japanese
Course Type: Sociolinguistics, Culture

Contextualization of topic

This course aims to prepare students for a meaningful short-term study abroad program (hereafter SA) by examining representative terms, key cultural concepts, and sociolinguistic/sociocultural aspects in the Japanese language that provide an insight into the social hierarchy, interpersonal relationships, and Japanese behavior, which consequently influence communication. Developed for students with little to no background in the language, the course offers a variety of resources and activities designed to increase an awareness and understanding of the relationship between Japanese language and culture in order to enhance students' intercultural communication and adjustment skills.

Course logistics

This course offers 3 credit hours applicable toward major requirements or free electives. It was offered in the spring semester concurrently with a similarly designed Korean course and culminated in a short-term (24 days) SA to Japan and Korea. The course included a 2-hour orientation, four 4-hour pre-departure meetings (scheduled on Saturdays), in-country class meetings, and a 2-hour post-trip debriefing.

Course objectives

ASIA 4490 objectives aim at nurturing global citizens better able to succeed in the 21st century, including

- Gaining a deeper knowledge and understanding of one's own and another culture
- Developing different perspectives in regard to another country
- Acquiring an increased respect for and tolerance of differences
- Learning to act in a manner that is appropriate in the host culture

These objectives and goals of the course support the Department's mission of "facilitating an understanding of human interaction across world cultures and time, [and] enhancing awareness of global perspectives," and the University's commitment to global understanding, mutual respect, and appreciation of human and cultural diversity.

Learning outcomes

Students will

- Identify and define cultural factors that play critical roles in the way Japanese people interact and communicate
- Recognize and define cultural dimensions that affect behavior and communication in Japanese
- Demonstrate a heightened awareness in communicating (verbally and nonverbally) and interacting effectively across cultures

Curricular structure

Due to the limited number of face-to-face class meetings, once a month for four months prior to SA departure, the course heavily utilized the flipped classroom approach, where instructional content is delivered online, outside of the classroom. Students were expected to spend 3–5 hours per week on outside readings, film viewings, online assignments, etc.

Students' grades were calculated as follows:

(30%) Attendance: orientation, pre-departure meetings, in-country excursions, debriefings, and post-trip meeting
(15%) Participation: Participation in discussions on readings, films, and inventories, both in face-to-face class sessions and online posts
(15%) Quizzes and Assignments: Content-related quizzes on readings and films; assignments (including inventories and film worksheets) both in-class and online submission posts
(20%) Journal: In-country daily entries (narrative text and digital pictures) of observations, interactions and activities including description, reflection, interpretation, and analysis

(20%) Final Projects:
- Post-trip video: a 10–15-min. video integrating SA experiences with course content, specifically key sociocultural concepts
- Paper: 5–7 pages, comparing 1–2 key cultural concepts of both Japanese and Korean cultures based on observations, explorations, and in-country experiences while integrating them with course content

Theoretical framework

Thematic in nature, the course begins by exploring key sociolinguistic and sociocultural concepts related to Japan from a global perspective:

- individualism vs. collectivism
- *uchi* (in-group)/*soto* (out-group)
- *shuudan ishiki* (group consciousness)
- *enryo* (mannerly restraint)

It then moves to Japanese communication style, delving into the functions of

- *aimai* (ambiguity)
- *haragei* (implicit exchange of thoughts and feelings)
- *honne* (private, true self) vs. *tatemae* (public persona)

Finally, it examines the abundantly rich theme of the individual:

- *giri* (social obligation) vs. *ninjo* (human feeling)
- *omoiyari* (thinking of others)
- *kenkyo* (modesty)
- *gaman* (endurance)
- *awase* (compromise)

Carefully chosen key concepts were intended to pique students' interest and demonstrate how these pragmatic features of Japanese language could be relevant to their language learning and subsequent preparation for their SA experience.

Teaching materials

Textbooks

- *The Japanese Mind: Understanding Contemporary Japanese Culture*, Roger J. Davies and Osamu Ikeno (Eds.), 2002

- Japanese Culture and Communication: Critical Cultural Analysis, Ray T. Donahue, 1998
- Understanding Japanese Society, Joy Hendry, 2012
- An Introduction to Japanese Society, Yoshio Sugimoto, 2010

Documentaries

- Kōkōyakyū: High School Baseball, Kenneth Eng, 2006
- A Life in Japan, Petri Storlöpare, 2013

Websites

- Strategies for Learning Speech Acts in Japanese http://carla.umn.edu/speechacts/japanese/introtospeechacts/index.htm

Class activities

➢ Pre-departure
The course begins with a 2-hour orientation outlining the course requirements, schedule, syllabus, in-country itinerary, service learning project, and a Japanese-to-English multiple choice pretest of the terms for the core cultural concepts comprising the focal points of the course. Interwoven into the pragmatics-centered curriculum were readings and activities dedicated to enriching students' language and cultural learning during their SA experience, specifically, materials that would promote their acculturation process with the overarching goal of enhancing their intercultural competence. This included readings and self-administered inventories from the guide on maximizing SAs, by Page et al. (2002), beginning with the Intensity Index to evaluate the emotional intensity of the SA program, and the degree of ethnocentricity of the SA participants, to the various readings on core cultural values, cross-cultural adjustment, and culture shock, as well as numerous language-learning strategies and inventories. As keeping a daily journal was a requirement for the SA portion of this course, the curriculum also included a "how-to" on journaling— not only for recording experiences and providing a reference for culture and language learning, but also as a means of learning about themselves and coping with emotions while in-country.

➢ SA (in-country)
The coursework laid the foundation for the short-term (12-day) SA to Japan (Tokyo, Kyoto, Osaka, and Nagoya), which included visits to famous sites, excursions to museums, traditional craft making and other experiential activities, and a day trip to a sister

institution, where students carried out their service learning project, engaging faculty and students in a language and culture exchange via a presentation introducing our university and the typical life of American college students. At a welcome party hosted by our sister institution, students put to the test their knowledge and practical application of the key sociocultural concepts focused on in their pre-departure, while forging international friendships as they communicated in both English and Japanese.

Finally, in-country group discussions were held allowing students time to decompress and explore their various phases and degrees of cultural awareness and adjustment. It was also an opportunity to encourage them to appreciate differences and remind them to be tolerant of any ambiguity they were experiencing in their respective acculturation processes, and not let language barriers become obstacles to a deeper understanding of the behaviors of the Japanese people and society.

From Japan, the SA continued in Korea, where students spent the next 12 days following a similar itinerary. Again, through direct immersion, students had the opportunity to compare Korean core cultural concepts with those of the Japanese, and gain an insight into how they are reflected in the ways of thinking, living, and communicating of the people of both countries.

➢ Post-trip
A 2-hour post-trip debriefing was held after returning from the SA, where a posttest of the core cultural concepts administered during orientation was again conducted. The debriefing also provided a space for reflecting on expectations of the course and SA program, met and unmet goals, and expressing thoughts and emotions around reentry and readaptation. An association game allowed students to spontaneously express their reactions to terms such as *gaman* (endurance), *wa* (harmony), and *enryo* (mannerly restraint). In addition, a haiku-writing activity tapped into their creative side as they expressed in 17 syllables the highlights of their heightened cultural awareness and discoveries, as seen in these two samples:

one empty train seat	rush-hour train stations
enryo no katamari *	*shuudan ishiki* **
I'll ride standing, too	waves of commuters
(Anonymous)	(Anonymous)
* the epitome of restraint	** group consciousness

Finally, students were encouraged to package their Japan experience by marketing their cross-cultural skills on their resumes and in job interviews. They were urged also to continue their international experience by enrolling or furthering their studies in a Japanese language and culture course at the university, to join and support the on-campus Japanese Club, and to seek out Japan-related organizations and events in the local community (Table 7.1).

Table 7.1 Sample Lesson Plan

Time	Activity	Sample Language
20 min. (during class)	In groups, conduct DAE (Describe, Analyze, Evaluate) activity with photos of Japanese scenes (e.g., woman covering mouth). Group discussion. Goal: develop awareness, increase empathy; demonstrate how cross-cultural misunderstandings can occur	*hazukashii* (shyness); *kenson/kenkyo* (modesty)
15 min. (outside of class)	Read selected pages of The Anatomy of Self (Doi); "The *DŌ* Spirit of Japan" and "*Gambari*: Japanese Patience and Determination" (from Davies and Ikeno's The Japanese Mind)	*dō* (the way/path); *gaman* (perseverance); *omoiyari* (thinking of others)
75 min. (outside of class) 20 min. (during class)	View *Kōkōyakyū* (High School Baseball); complete worksheet; Group discussion. Goal: heighten conscious awareness of pragmatic norms. Lecture: permeation of these cultural terms in everyday life	
15 min. (outside of class)	Internet search: Find an article to share with the class that explores the concept of *seishin* found within business, sports, or some other aspect of everyday life	*seishin* (spirit/heart)
20 min. (during class)	Individual presentations	
10 min. (outside of class)	http://carla.umn.edu/speechacts/japanese/introtospeechacts/index.htm Complete 1–2 speech-act vignettes	*sumimasen* (Thanks/Sorry/Excuse me); *sore-wa-chotto-muzukashii* (That's a bit difficult); *kono-mae-wa-doomo* (Thanks for the other day)
15 min. (during class)	Group discussion of results. Goals: enhance strategies for learning speech acts in Japanese, promote pragmatic self-awareness raising tasks, provide sociocultural information	

Ideas for future class activities

Ideas for course enhancement include

- Increase in technology use for content presentation and assessments (e.g., Edpuzzle, Vizia, LearningApps, etc.)
- Stronger component of elementary-level expressions (e.g., *os*, *ohayoo* and *ohayoo gozaimasu* demonstrating the hierarchy of Japanese society)
- Addition of short video clips from Japanese TV dramas to expose students to language and cultural concepts
- Addition of news and online articles

Evaluation

Student evaluations were based on the grading scale listed under Curricular Structure. Attendance at all meetings, excursions, and debriefings were mandatory as was active participation in class discussions, group activities, and online postings. Formative assessments included multiple-choice, matching, and short-answer quizzes on readings and films, and assignments such as inventories and film-related worksheets. Additionally, a peer collaborative presentation was also assigned in which pairs of students researched a cultural topic (e.g., body language, pop culture, eating and drinking establishments, temples, and shrines) and posted on the online discussion board summaries of central elements comparing that cultural aspect in both Japanese and Korean cultures. Students then read all summaries and commented on at least two other topics. The main in-country formative assessment was the daily journal, the requirements of which included both narrative text and digital pictures, and was evaluated on demonstration of description, reflection, interpretation, and analysis.

Summative assessments focused on in-country service-learning projects consisting of group presentations, and a two-part final project: a post-trip video and a paper. Students were allowed artistic license with the video and were encouraged to exercise creativity and originality as they integrated their SA experiences with the key sociocultural concepts they had focused on in pre-SA discussions and in-country debriefings. In their 5–7-page paper, students were required to select one or two cultural concepts of both Japanese and Korean cultures, comparing their manifestations in daily lives and communication styles. The criteria on which the papers were evaluated were length, depth of interpretation and analysis, and demonstration of an integration of course content. Rubrics for the projects were detailed during the orientation at the beginning of the course.

Caveats and reflections

One of the many strengths of this course is its offering within a SA program, as both have overlapping goals and objectives related to intercultural competence. Research has found that studying abroad has become a useful strategy in developing and shaping intercultural competence (Andrews and Henze), and an understanding of key sociocultural concepts via instruction targeting pragmatic features of Japanese may lead to unlocking the door to communication by equipping students with information that would benefit them in interacting with Japanese appropriately and avoiding violating social and cultural rules. This course could, nevertheless, be easily adapted, expanded, and offered as a full-semester humanities course independent of a SA program.

The flipped classroom environment is also a strength. Such format promotes student-centered instruction that allows students to come to class prepared for activities and discussions, leading to a more engaging setting with more time to interact with classmates and the instructor (Davis).

In addition, the deeply rooted relationship that exists between language and culture cannot be disputed, and central to the process of learning another language is understanding this relationship. However, many beginning foreign language courses and textbooks, Japanese included, often begin with the nuts and bolts of language such as vocabulary, expressions, grammar, and writing systems, before or without introducing students to language in its cultural framework. ASIA 4490 offers a unique introduction to foreign (Japanese) language learning as it emphasizes students' development of an awareness of the ways in which Japanese sociolinguistic and sociocultural concepts (e.g., modesty, vagueness, compromise) interrelate with the language, thereby influencing how they create and interpret meaning—what Shively refers to as "TL pragmatic competence." Cross-listed with other humanities courses, this course has the potential of attracting students looking beyond foreign language department offerings.

Suggestions for adapting this course for such future offerings include its separation from a SA program and offering it as a semester-long stand-alone course. The possibilities for course expansion then become limitless, with additional activities and content that ideally would include guest speakers, authentic sources (e.g., commercials, songs, advertisements), and other computer-mediated resources. Furthermore, developing a more robust language component could strengthen its fulfillment of a foreign language requirement.

ASIA 4490 takes a sociolinguistic approach to learning the Japanese language by developing an understanding of the human culture, social behavior and interpersonal relationships, and communication of the

Japanese via an exploration of core cultural concepts. The benefits of approaching foreign language study from this sociocultural, sociolinguistic perspective may have great implications and in the long term could produce foreign language learners with increased skills in intercultural communication. If an overarching goal in our foreign language classrooms is to nurture students to becoming global citizens with enhanced intercultural competence, the possibility of unlocking doors to communication with the key of understanding sociocultural concepts may well be worth exploring.

References

Andrews, Deborah C., and Brent Henze. "Teaching Professional Writing to American Students in a Study Abroad Program." *Business Communication Quarterly*, vol. 72, 2009, pp. 5–20.
Davis, Nicole L. "Anatomy of a Flipped Classroom." *Journal of Teaching in Travel and Tourism*, vol. 16, no. 3, 2016, pp. 228–232.
Page, R. Michael et al. *Maximizing Study Abroad: A Students' Guide to Strategies for Language and Culture Learning and Use*. University of Minnesota Center for Advanced Research on Language Acquisition, 2002.
Shively, Rachel L. "From the Virtual World to the Real World: A Model of Pragmatics Instruction for Study Abroad." *The Foreign Language Annals*, vol. 43, no.1, 2010, pp. 105–137.

Teaching material references

A Life in Japan. Directed by Petri Storlöpare. 2013. YouTube.
Center for Advanced Research on Language Acquisition (CARLA). *Strategies for Learning Speech Acts in Japanese*. Accessed 12 February 2019. carla.umn.edu/speechacts/japanese/introtospeechacts/index.htm.
Davies, Roger J., and Osamu Ikeno, eds. *The Japanese Mind: Understanding Contemporary Japanese Culture*. Tuttle Publishing, 2002.
Donahue, Ray T. *Japanese Culture and Communication: Critical Cultural Analysis*. University Press of America, 1998.
Hendry, Joy. *Understanding Japanese Society*. Nissan Institute/Routledge Japanese Studies, 2012.
Kōkōyakyū: High School Baseball. Directed by Kenneth Eng. PBS-POV, 2006.
Sugimoto, Yoshio. *An Introduction to Japanese Society*. Cambridge University Press, 2010.

Suggested supplemental teaching material references

Doi, Takeo. *The Anatomy of Self: The Individual vs. Society*. Kodansha International, 2001.
Gung Ho. Directed by Ron Howard, Paramount Pictures, 1986.

Henshall, Kenneth G. *Dimensions of Japanese Society: Gender, Margins and Mainstreams*. St. Martin's Press, Inc., 1999.

Lebra, Takie Sugiyama, and William P. Lebra, eds. *Japanese Culture and Behavior: Selected Readings*. University of Hawaii Press, 1986.

Like Father, Like Son. Directed by Hirokazu Kore-eda. Amuse, 2013.

Tokyo Sonata. Directed by Kiyoshi Kurosawa. Hakuhodo-DY Media Partners, 2009.

8 Approaching language issues critically: language in Japanese society

Rika Ito

Course Title: ASIAN 126: Language in Japanese Society
Course Level: Introductory, open to all students
Language(s) in Focus: Japanese
Course Type: Asian Studies, Linguistics, Sociocultural Linguistics

Contextualization of topic

Learning a language in the context of culture and society is essential. In Japanese, even a simple greeting requires an understanding of the appropriate level of formality. Students encounter gendered language in all speech styles ranging from informal to honorific registers. Japanese textbooks tend to present an essentialized view of Japanese language and culture—a homogeneous, hierarchical, and gendered society that is embedded in language use. These prescribed descriptions reproduce a *nihonjinron* discourse (theories about what it means to be Japanese) despite the fact that *nihonjinron* has been widely criticized in academia (Befu). Against this backdrop, important scholarly works have emerged that critically examine the regimentation of Japanese in the context of the creation of modern state: standardization of the language (Lee), honorifics (Wetzel), and women's language (Inoue, Nakamura). In the field of pedagogy, various scholars propose critical approaches to teaching Japanese and culture (e.g., Kubota, Sato et al.). Other scholars examine the hegemony of English in the context of globalization (e.g., Kachru). Reflecting these developments, this course critically examines language usage in Japanese society.

Course logistics

This is a 1-credit-hour course that meets for 55 min. three times a week. There is no prerequisite. The course counts toward both Asian Studies and Japanese majors, and Linguistics Studies concentration (similar to minor in other institutions). The course also fulfills three General Education requirements: Multicultural Studies-Global, Oral Communication, and Studies in Human Behaviors and Society.

Course objectives

This introductory-level course explores the major sociocultural aspects of language use in Japan. Students will critically examine the role of language in society by analyzing the writing system, loanwords, pronoun systems, regional dialects, and gender differences, along with a few key cultural concepts (in-group/out-group and vertical relationship). The course will also review the historical, social, and ideological background of the creation of "women's language" and its implications within a contemporary context.

Learning outcomes

By the end of the semester, students are able to

- Identify several characteristics of Japanese language structures and usage and how they relate to the cultural and social conventions of Japan
- Explain the gap between the conventions and actual language practices in a critical manner
- Problematize the reproduction of linguistic stereotypes in media
- Compare and contrast language use in Japan with their own culture
- Discuss issues of language ideologies in Japan
- Demonstrate confidence and effectiveness in oral communication skills

Curricular structure

This course was developed using a backward design approach. I identified the intended learning outcomes first, then determined assessment tools, and finally arranged materials most appropriate for learning experiences as lesson plans. The course format is a combination of mini-lectures, small group/class discussions, and student presentations.

Evaluation criteria are as follows:

(10%) Class attendance/participation
(10%) Reading response
(10%) Mini-presentations in small groups

(5%) Group discussion leadership
(20%) Sociolinguistic lab reports
(25%) Final project
(20%) Final exam (take-home)

Theoretical framework

The class promotes active learning. Students are asked to engage actively in the learning process through various means such as small group and class discussions, and submitting questions and discussion prompts prior to class. Interaction with others enables students to share different ideas and perspectives, thus, fostering collaborative learning and critical thinking. The course is also project-based. Students learn about sociocultural linguistics by conducting a sociocultural project, which incorporates various scholarly work and class discussions. To facilitate critical thinking, reading materials are carefully selected to illustrate the differences among grammatical rules (i.e., conventions), actual language practices, and language ideologies.

Teaching materials

Gender, Language, and Ideology: A Genealogy of Japanese Women's Language, Momoko Nakamura, 2014.
A complete list may be found in the References section.

Class activities

I start the course with selected chapters from books directed to a general audience. I also assign readings that outline the history of Japan and the development of the Japanese language. After laying this foundation, the course is organized by themes such as writing systems, loanwords, and reference terms (i.e., pronouns). Toward the end of the semester, we read Nakamura (2014) as a case study to explore how language has functioned as a proxy to confine women throughout history from the *Kamakura* Period (late 12th century) to the present. A group of students present the main point of the readings and lead class discussions. Below I present my lesson plans and activities for the topic related to reference terms in Japanese, focusing on the English equivalent of *you* and *I*.

> Section One
> On the first day, the grammatical rules are presented. I assign multiple readings: a table summarizing reference terms in Japanese, a

chapter titled "Japanese Speakers Avoid Certain Pronouns," and a book chapter titled "Words for Self and Other."

First, I present a slide of the Makino and Tsutsui's summary table: Japanese equivalent of English *you* and *I* have multiple forms depending on the formality and the gender of the speaker. Then I ask the following questions to check students' comprehension:

- How many factors are involved in deciding a self-reference term?
- Which ones are recommended to avoid?

➤ Section Two

I briefly explain the avoidance of pronouns, particularly the equivalent of *you* (*anata, omae,* and *kisama*) in Japanese. For example, *kisama* 貴様 (literally "noble you") went through a drastic semantic and pragmatic change: from expressing respect in the past to a vulgar expression, commonly used in a fighting scene such as students may have seen in *anime*.

➤ Section Three

Next, we move on to the main part of the class: understanding Suzuki's analysis of the systematicity of Japanese reference terms. I display two key figures from his chapter: one on various terms for *you* and *I* represented by a hypothetical middle-aged man in various contexts, and another on the use of kinship terms as a pronoun in a family tree format. Students discuss how the chart illustrates the systematicity of the kinship terms to address family members in pairs. After a short discussion, I show a short *anime* clip (*Chi's Sweet Homes*) to illustrate the use of *okāsan* "mom" by a husband to address his wife. I also ask students to compare and contrast the use of kinship terms in Japanese and their own culture. I briefly explain two different sets of Chinese characters for *oji* "uncles": one for older siblings of your parents (伯父) and the other one for younger siblings (叔父) whose distinction is lost for most Japanese these days. I also point out a semantic bias in *kyōdai* 兄弟: while the term is a compound of "older brother" and "younger brother," it also refers to female siblings as unmarked "siblings."

➤ Section Four

In the final segment of the class, I use the movie, *Kimi no na wa (Your Name)*, as a case study. The main plot concerns the swapping of bodies between a teenage boy and a girl; there are a few comical scenes at the beginning of the movie when these two do not behave as expected. In one particular scene, when the girl is in the body of the boy with his close friends, she uses *watashi* "I" (used by both men and women in a formal setting or women in general), which puzzles his friends. She also uses a series of "I" in Japanese: *watakushi* (very formal), *boku*, and finally *ore*. I also present a *manga* version on a slide because it is easier to track the various forms of "I" in Japanese. For a small group discussion, I pose reflective questions to the students such as:

- Whether those without a knowledge of the Japanese language would be lost in translation due to the subtle nuance expressed in these terms, and
- Whether the Japanese pronoun system has an advantage or disadvantage compared to English (or other languages that they speak)

We also explore language practices by real people such as the lesbian, gay, bisexual, transgender, queer (LGBTQ) community, middle school students, and young children. Students read only one of the three selections. In class, students work in a small group with those who have read different readings to compare and contrast the content of the readings by using a jigsaw method. In the class discussion, students are asked to reflect on how their language use is related to their own identities. The subsequent two classes are designated for various representations as seen in media.

For each class period, students must submit reflections, questions, or discussion prompts, regarding the reading before each class period by using a "Forum" on *Moodle*, a free online course management system. This also allows me to adjust the content of my mini-lecture as needed.

In order to complement classroom discussion, I assign several *sociolinguistic lab reports* in which students apply the analytical perspectives discussed in the readings by observing various popular media. Students will submit a one-page report (approximately 500 words). For example, when discussing reference terms, students have two choices:

- Watch either *Your Name* to observe how one character is referred differently by using Suzuki and reflect on whether those who don't know Japanese can be lost in translation
- Watch selected episodes of *Cowboy Bebop* to complement Hiramoto's study that problematizes visual and linguistic representation of gender hegemony

In this way, the class materials and activities are meaningfully integrated while individual analysis and reflection are promoted. The lab reports also prepare students for their final project. (See below for details.)

Evaluation

Every assessment is formative, except for the final exam. Below, I will describe the final project in detail. The last component of the course is a formal individual presentation (10 min. with Q/A) at our Mini-Sociocultural Linguistic Conference on Language and Society at the end of the semester, usually 4–5 days.

The goal of the final project is to integrate students' understanding of issues of language in society, examined in the course, by conducting original research. Any aspects of language and society that concern language use and/or language ideologies can be presented, thus, students may analyze languages other than Japanese. A project must be based on mini-data observation using various media (e.g., movies, music, *anime*, games) and analyzing it using at least three relevant scholarly sources, including the ones assigned in class, as a point of reference. Students may employ either quantitative or qualitative analysis, or both. Many pursue something very tangible such as the use of English, variation in written Japanese, gendered language, or *keigo*. Some of the actual topics include the following:

- The use of English, Japanese, and Korean in J-pop and K-pop
- The use of *katakana* and English in J-pop titles
- The representation of foreigners in the *anime, Gintama*
- The language representation of LGBTQ characters in the *anime, Wandering Son*
- The representation of bad girls in a TV drama

To create a formal, professional atmosphere, I distribute a program similar to those distributed at professional conferences. The program includes the presenters' names, the titles of the presentations, short abstracts (50 words), and 3–5 keywords. I also assign a student to be a moderator who introduces the speaker, notifies the speaker of the remaining time with flashcards, and moderates the Q/A session.

For this final project, there are four steps that build on each other:

- Project Brainstorming: Students will submit a paragraph to describe a project. They are encouraged to brainstorm and discuss ideas with me before the deadline.
- Prospectus: Students will submit a 1–1.5-page prospectus that describes what they will investigate, why, and what they plan to accomplish in the study, as well as an annotated bibliography that

includes at least three entries. Grading criteria are based on a general understanding of the context and purpose for writing, clarity of the goal of the project, the relevance of the sources and evaluation, and language control and mechanics.
- Presentation Abstract and Short Abstract (with keywords): Students will submit a 500-word summary of their presentation. It should be concrete and concise and address the following: the goal of the project, previous studies to contextualize the project, data and methodology, preliminary results and interpretation. Grading is based on the clarity/catchiness of the title, a general understanding of the context, the quality of the literature review, the clarity of the goal of the project, the adequateness of data, methodology, the description of results, analysis, and language control and mechanics.
- In-class Presentation: Each student has 15 min. Grading is based on the clarity of the central message, organization, contextualization, findings, relevance/significance, supporting visual aids, language, and delivery. Three to four students evaluate the presentation along with the instructor.

Caveats and reflections

Students tend to view grammar as a set of fixed right-or-wrong rules, especially in the context of language learning. This course opens up an opportunity for students to critically view language through the examination of mismatch between the grammar explained in the textbooks and actual language practices, as well as the influence of ideology in linguistic descriptions. Students also systematically examine language represented in popular media. This new perspective seems to motivate students to continue their language study. Additionally, providing a perspective and vocabulary to talk critically about language matters is one of the strengths of this course. A class taught in English that includes foreign language content creates opportunities to discuss difficult issues regarding equity and diversity, often disguised as language issues. For example, students learn that women were belittled and confined by their language throughout history. By juxtaposing the situation of Japanese women and that of women in the current US, students can see similar problems that women face. Language awareness in the context of society and power structure is extremely relevant in the current divisive climate toward women and minorities.

References

Befu, Harumi. "Nationalism and Nihonjinron." *Cultural Nationalism in East Asia: Representation and Identity*, edited by Harumi Befu, Institute of East Asian Studies, University of California, 1993, pp. 107–135.

Inoue, Miyako. *Vicarious Language: Gender and Linguistic Modernity in Japan*. University of California Press, 2006.

Kachru, Braj B. "The Power and Politics of English." *World Englishes*, vol. 5, no. 2–3, 1986, pp. 121–140.

Kubota, Ryuko. "Japanese Culture Constructed by Discourses: Implications for Applied Linguistics Research and ELT." *TESOL Quarterly*, vol. 33, no. 1, 1999, pp. 9–35.

Lee, Yeounsuk. *The Ideology of Kokugo: Nationalizing Language in Modern Japan*. University of Hawaii Press, 2010.

Sato, Shinji et al., eds. *Language Education for Social Future: Critical Content-Based Instruction*. Coco Publisher, 2015.

Wetzel, Patricia J. *Keigo in Modern Japan: Polite Language from Meiji to the Present*. University of Hawai'i Press, 2004.

Teaching material references

Abe, Hideko. "Lesbian Bar Talk in Shinjuku, Tokyo." *Japanese Language, Gender, and Ideology: Cultural Models and Real People*, edited by Shigeko Okamoto and Janet S. Shibamoto Smith, Oxford University Press, 2004, pp. 205–221.

"Chi, motomeru [Chi, on the prowl]." *Chi's Sweet Home: atarashī ouchi [Chi's Sweet Home: Chi's New Address]*, TXN (TV Tokyo), 30 March 2009.

Cipris, Zeljko, and Shoko Hamano. *Making Sense of Japanese Grammar a Clear Guide through Common Problems*. University of Hawaii Press, 2002.

Cowboy Bebop: The Perfect Sessions, directed by Shinichiro Watanabe, Bandai Entertainment, 2001.

Hiramoto, Mie. "Hey, You're a Girl?: Gendered Expressions in the Popular Anime, Cowboy Bebop." *Multilingua*, vol. 32, no. 1, 2013, pp. 51–78.

Ito, Rika. "Boku or Watashi: Variation in Self-Reference Terms among Japanese Children." *Innovation and Continuity in Language and Communication of Different Language Cultures*, edited by Rudolf Muhr and Richard Schrodt, Peter Lang Publishing, 2006. pp. 123–142.

Kimi no na wa (Your name). Directed by Makoto Shinkai, Toho, 2016.

Makino, Seiichi, and Michio Tsutsui. *A Dictionary of Basic Japanese Grammar*. Japan Times, 1986.

Miyazaki, Ayumi. "Japanese Junior High School Girls' and Boys' First-Person Pronoun Use and Their Social World." *Japanese Language, Gender, and Ideology: Cultural Models and Real People*, edited by Shigeko Okamoto and Janet S. Shibamoto Smith, Oxford University Press, 2004, pp. 256–274.

Nakamura, Momoko. *Gender, Language, and Ideology: A Genealogy of Japanese Women's Language*. John Benjamins Publishing Company, 2014.
Robertson, Wesley. "He's More Katakana than Kanji: Indexing Identity and Self-Presentation through Script Selection in Japanese Manga (Comics)." *Journal of Sociolinguistics*, vol. 21, no. 4, 2017, pp. 497–520.
Suzuki, Takao. *Words in Context: A Japanese Perspective on Language and Culture*. Translated by Akira Miura, Kodansha International, 2001.

9 Japanese sociolinguistics: Reacting to the Past and beyond

Noriko Akimoto Sugimori

Course Title: JAPN 245 Japanese Language in Society
Course Level: Introductory
Language(s) in Focus: Japanese
Course Type: Sociolinguistics, Japanese history, Japanese society

Contextualization of topic

Japanese Language in Society, an introductory sociolinguistics course, is part of the culture course offerings for the East Asian Studies major. Sociolinguistics is a branch of linguistics research that studies the relationship between language and society. This course covers topics, such as language variations, politeness, gender, language ideology, and language policy.

The background for this course consists of the Japanese language, modern Japanese history, and theory of language ideology or people's beliefs about language. Makino and Tsutsui (1989) and Gottlieb (2005) have described the characteristics of Japanese grammar and writing system, including the use of four orthographies—*hiragana* such as さとう, *katakana* such as サトウ, *kanji* (Chinese characters) such as 砂糖, and the Roman alphabet.

The Meiji Restoration in 1868 marked the end of samurai rule and the beginning of Japan's modern period. Japan's first daily newspapers appeared in the early 1870s. Therefore, to augment understanding of major historical events, including World War II and the Allied occupation, several physical copies of newspapers are shown to the class for a discussion of social change and language use. Such class demonstrations explain social meanings behind the orthographic choice. For example, it takes years to master *kanji*, but not to learn *hiragana* and *katakana*. Replacing *kanji* with *hiragana* was associated with making the language more accessible to the public, which is the democratization of the language. It was also associated with Japan's separation from China. Shifting language ideologies underpin changes in language use.

Course logistics

This 3.33-credit-hour course is taught face-to-face and is designed to be accessible to students with no prior background in linguistics. Previous Japanese language learning is recommended, but not required. The class meets for 75 min., three times a week, for ten weeks, on a quarter system. The course counts as an elective for the completion of East Asian Studies major and as a general elective.

Course objectives

This sociolinguistic course explores topics such as language variations, politeness, gender differences, and language ideology. The goal of this course is to enhance students' knowledge of and sensitivity to the intercultural and sociolinguistic factors that contribute to the construction of everyday interaction and discourse in mass media, and translation.

Learning outcomes

By the end of the quarter, students will be able to

- Identify several characteristics of Japanese language structures and usage and their relation to historical developments of the language
- Explain the difference between the prescription and description of language
- Problematize the reproduction of linguistic stereotypes in the media
- Critically examine language use in Japanese as well as in their native language(s)
- Discuss some issues of language ideologies that are operative at macro and micro levels

Curricular structure

This course is structured using backward design, in which the teaching materials are given to attain the course's goal, that is, to enhance students' knowledge of and sensitivity to the intercultural and sociolinguistic aspects of Japanese. Grades are based on

(15%) Class participation
(25%) Online discussion
(10%) Leading reading discussions
(5%) Refresher
(10%) Interview project paper
(15%) Role-play
(20%) Final project paper

Theoretical framework

The course is designed to enhance students' understanding of the relationship between language and society. This is accomplished by connecting language issues at the micro level (e.g., individual language use) with language issues at the macro level (e.g., national level of language policy making). After providing the necessary background, such as basic Japanese grammar and writing system, the course introduces Irvine and Gal's (2000) theory of semiotic processes of language ideology. This theory explains how semiotic processes, such as "erasure," operate in the formation of language ideology. For example, in the formation of national language, the speakers' bilingualism was "erased." The language ideology connects the macro and micro phenomena. After learning about grammar, writing system, and language ideology, the course covers the following three thematic units: regional differences in pitch and accent, gender differences in pronoun use and pronunciation, and English education. Challenges in translating between English and Japanese are also discussed throughout the course.

The course moves to macro level issues through an overview of the modern history of Japanese language planning. Attention is paid to the roles of certain language planners, and the students engage in Reacting to the Past (RTTP) role-play. RTTP is a game pedagogy in undergraduate history education that has proven effective in engaging students. In RTTP, students assume the roles of historical figures, informed by authentic classical texts in elaborate games that are set in various epochs such as the French Revolution. Generally, instructors use RTTP materials, published or intended for RTTP publication. Students read primary sources in preparing to play the roles of historical figures. Rather than having students re-enact historical events, RTTP, which does not use a fixed script or expect a given outcome, invites students to embrace "historical tensions, conflict, and controversy as key to the pedagogy" and "through deep study and participation in acts of written and verbal persuasion" (RTTP Publications Committee 2016, Barnard College 2019). In other words, students play roles to persuade others to accept their argument. In this way, they demonstrate an understanding of the relationship between language and society.

Teaching materials

Books

- *Language and Society in Japan*, Nanette Gottlieb, 2005
- *The Making of Monolingual Japan: Language Ideology and Japanese Modernity*, Patrick Heinrich, 2012
- *What Is Sociolinguistics?* Gerard Van Herk, 2017

Films

- *Karera ga honki de amutoki wa* [*Close-Knit*], Naoko Ogigami, 2017
- *Kimi no na wa.* [*Your Name.*], Makoto Shinkai, 2016
- *Okoge* [*Fag Hag*], Takehiro Nakajima, 1992

Class activities

The following is a description of a sample lesson that focuses on RTTP role-play with discrete language use. After the ground rules of the role-playing game are explained, students pretend to be actual language policy makers from the past who have a discussion. Each student receives a role sheet and does research on his or her assigned role. Most of these roles are prominent policy makers for modern Japanese. The students then discuss the direction of the Japanese language in the 21st century.

Students develop their roles based on class readings by Heinrich (2012) and on other materials from their own research. Heinrich describes present and past discrepancies in Japan's modern language policy through the lens of sociolinguistics. To catch up with the West, Japan began to make deliberate efforts toward modernization by spreading the ideology of a unitary language (*kokugo*) based on practices in Western nations. Heinrich's book challenges the myth of Japan as a monolingual country.

There were four major figures who promoted the idea of *kokugo* in the making of Japan's language policy. In addition, I created several fictional roles such as a Japanese teacher of English, an American teacher of English in Japan, and linguistics professors who specialize in minority languages in Okinawa and Ainu.

- (5 min.) Explanation of Course-specific Ground Rules
  Although the course discussion is held in English, students are instructed to follow Japanese communication rules. More specifically, the Japanese language allows for longer pauses than the English language. In addition, when it comes to taking turns speaking, turns are distributed more equitably in Japanese. To encourage participation by international students in the class who are nonnative English speakers, these students are given small flags. When they wave a flag, they may take their turn and their comments cannot be cut off by the other students. These course-specific rules make the students experience a communication style that is closer to that of the Japanese language.
- (20 min.) Self-introduction and Speech
  All presenters (language policy makers) take turns introducing themselves and their positions on the future of the Japanese language. They also express their views about the introduction of English in elementary school and the use of *kanji* characters.
- (40 min.) Q/A and Discussion
  Students respond to the specific points that other students raised by asking questions. Students debate the points raised by a presenter or by other students.
- (10 min.) Feedback by the Instructor and Students
  The instructor comments on each student's performance and provides information about present-day national language policy meetings, directing the students' attention to differences between real language policy makers and the roles they played. The students vote for the student who gave the most convincing performance and write down the reason, providing a rationale for their choices.

Activities beyond RTTP

Regional differences

The theme of regional differences in language use is introduced through an experiential component such as student interviews of native and near-native speakers of Japanese outside the classroom. Students record their pronunciations of ten short Japanese expressions, including *kaze-ga* [wind-nominative] and *tori-ga* [bird-nominative]. Then they record the informants' pronunciation of the same expressions, and compare the results with those appearing in Shibatani's book. When they find discrepancies, they explore why they occurred. The class discussion problematizes this method and discusses recent developments in web applications such as praat [talk], a software program for speech analysis in phonetics.

Gender differences

Gender differences in language use are discussed by using past research and films. I use all linguistic expressions encountered in this course as a source of discussion of their underlying social meanings, and I try to expand students' thinking about the idea of "language." For example, seemingly bland examples of Japanese grammar from a grammar dictionary become a valuable source of discussion on the recent historical shift in the description of women in Japan. Examples to explain grammar such as personal pronoun and passive include *Boku no kanojo, totemo kireina n da* [My girlfriend is very pretty, you know] (Makino and Tsutsui 32), and *Kimura-san wa bijin no yoko ni suwarete ureshi sōda* [Lit. Mr. Kimura, having a pretty woman sit beside him, looks happy] (33). In addition, the course discusses historical and cross-cultural shifts in the social meanings of orthography. Examples include women not being allowed to use Chinese characters in the 10th century and pitch accents as with Japanese female high-pitched "cute" voice in the original *anime* being lost in the *anime* that was translated into English.

Evaluation

Formative assessments (class participation, online discussion, reading discussion leader, and refresher) are provided to facilitate students' learning. The assessments are also important for the instructor to assess appropriate scaffolding. Summative assessments include the interview project paper, role-play, and the final project paper. The evaluation for the summative assessments is provided here.

In the interview project, students form groups consisting of 2–3 members and ask individuals who lived in Japan about their Japanese language acquisition experiences. The students ask them to pronounce ten Japanese phrases and compare the pitch accent patterns from the published results in the regions where the speakers lived. Students are graded by how well they explained the discrepancy between theory and practice. The role-play grade is determined by how accurately the students portray their roles in the RTTP activity.

The final project is to meet the needs of diverse students' interests and learning styles. Consequently, students choose from one of three options.

- Translation Project: Students find and explain reasons behind some discrepancies between Japanese *anime* in English and their Japanese originals. The paper is evaluated based on the depth of their analysis and how effectively they used the class materials in their discussion.
- Literature Review and Proposal Project: Students analyze at least two articles in academic journals in sociolinguistics and propose a study to make the research better. The paper is evaluated based on the accuracy in interpreting the data in the journal articles and the soundness of the proposed study.
- Free Sociolinguistic Topic: Students propose and conduct their study. They also write a rubric. Their paper and rubric are evaluated based on the soundness of the discussion.

Caveats and reflections

I think that there is always room to improve the introduction of the role-play component. Except for theatre majors, none of the students had engaged in this kind of a role-play before. When I introduced the role-play assignment for the first time, an international student from Asia complained that playing a role in a second language was very difficult. It was especially hard to participate in the discussion. The difficulty that some international students had with this task may not only be attributed to their limited proficiency in English. The assignment may have also been challenging if the students were not familiar with the principles of creative conflict or productive argumentation. For students who seem uncomfortable expressing their emotions or making an argument, as suggested in RTTP literature, it might be worthwhile to create neutral roles for them, such as "reporter" or "historian."

I introduced a simplified version of RTTP in my course. In the authentic RTTP class, students read more published primary sources that had survived RTTP's rigorous quality control and peer review. In the authentic RTTP, students may take on historic personas for several weeks, but my course covered this component in less than three. Therefore, my practice showed that a core idea of RTTP could be just as effective on a smaller scale. The authentic RTTP is not feasible for a sociolinguistics course because no teaching materials or "games" on this topic have been published. There are very few RTTP games devoted to themes from Japan. Some historians blame the complexities associated with translation of historical primary sources from East Asian languages into English, making the scarcity of East Asian RTTP materials a language-based problem.

RTTP discussions both helped my students acquire emic perspectives toward Japanese language use and to reexamine the use of their native languages. Creating some mechanism to engage students with limited English proficiency raised all the students' awareness of communication style differences between English and Japanese and reassured students with diverse backgrounds in the classroom. I am convinced that their learning of sociolinguistics in the Japanese contexts in this course has laid a foundation for successful communication in their mother tongues as well as in foreign languages in an increasingly globalized world.

References

"The Concept." *Reacting to the Past*. Barnard College. reacting.barnard.edu/reacting-home. Accessed 23 April 2019.

"RTTP Publications Committee Guidelines for Game Authors, Controversial Issues, 4th Draft." *Reacting to the Past*. Summer 2016. reacting.barnard.edu/development-resources. Accessed 9 April 2019.

Teaching Material References

Boersma, Paul, and David Weenink. "Praat: Doing Phonetics by Computer." www.fon.hum.uva.nl/praat/ 24 April 2019.

Gottlieb, Nanette. *Language and Society in Japan*. Cambridge University Press, 2005.

Heinrich, Patrick. *The Making of Monolingual Japan: Language Ideology and Japanese Modernity*. Multilingual Matters, 2012.

Irvine, Judith T., and Susan Gal. "Language Ideology and Linguistic Differentiation." *Regimes of Language: Ideologies, Politics, and Identities*, edited by Paul V. Kroskrity, School of American Research Press, 2000, pp. 35–84.

Karera ga honki de amutoki wa [Close-Knit], directed by Naoko Ogigami, 2017.

Kimi no na wa. [Your Name.], directed by Makoto Shinkai, 2016.

Makino, Seiichi, and Michio Tsutsui. "Characteristics of Japanese Grammar." *A Dictionary of Basic Japanese Grammar*. Japan Times, 1989, pp. 16–49.

Okoge [Fag Hag], directed by Takehiro Nakajima, 1992.

Shibatani, Masayoshi. *The Languages of Japan*. Cambridge University Press, 1990.

Van Herk, Gerard. *What Is Sociolinguistics?* Wiley Publications, 2017.

10 Language, identity, and power in Japan: gender in Japanese language

Junko Ueno

Course Title: MLT250 Language, Identity, and Power in Japan
Course Level: Lower-Division, open to all students
Language(s) in Focus: Japanese
Course Type: Linguistics, Gender Studies, Culture Studies

Contextualization of topic

Language and culture are inseparable entities, as they are closely intertwined with each other. This is a sociolinguistics course that studies the intimate relationships between people's verbal behaviors and social and cultural constructs. People tend to make different language choices that are considered appropriate depending on various social contexts based on cultural norms. These norms are closely related to linguistic ideology defined as "a rationalization of perceived language structure and use" (Silverstein 193). For instance, socially formulated gender identities could affect how men and women speak differently. While some may follow such normative linguistic practices, others may choose a divergent linguistic production depending on their linguistic identities. This course focuses on the establishment of one's verbal life based on one's linguistic identities in the context of Japan.

Course logistics

This course carries 4 credit hours. It counts toward an interdepartmental major or minor in Japanese. Students can also take it to fulfill a major, interdepartmental major or minor in the Asian Studies Program and the Gender, Sexuality, and Women's Studies Program. Additionally, it carries a languages and culture credit and writing across the curriculum credit in college's Common Curriculum requirements. There are no language prerequisites. The course is designed for face-to-face teaching. Classes meet three times a week for 65 min.

Course objectives

The goal of this course is to enhance students' cultural competency as global citizens. It exposes students to concepts and terminologies related to Japanese sociolinguistics and language. By doing so, it aims at developing students' understanding of the dynamic relationship between language use and cultural and social organizations.

Learning outcomes

At the end of the course, students will be able to

- Increase knowledge of Japanese culture through the Japanese language and its linguistics
- Improve their analytical skills by critically interpreting concepts in Japanese culture as compared to their own
- Improve their communication skills by working collaboratively in leading and participating discussions

Curricular structure

The course structure is based on class participation, short exercises, leading class discussions, short papers, a midterm examination, and a final paper. This is primarily a discussion-based class. A high level of oral participation is expected from all students. The evaluation criteria for the course are as follows:

(15%) Class participation
(5%) Short exercises
(10%) Leading class discussion
(20%) Short papers
(20%) Midterm examination
(30%) Final paper

Theoretical framework

The course loosely follows an inquiry-based learning approach as a theoretical framework. Justice et al. define inquiry-based learning as "instructional practices that promote student learning through student-driven and instructor-guided investigations of student-centered questions" (202). The instructor provides reading questions for each reading assignment designed to allow students to think about the issues related to the topic beforehand and actively engage themselves in class discussions. In addition to the reading questions, students have short exercises for which they submit their answers on the course website prior to the class. Thus, the class discussion is built upon their opinions and perspectives rather than the instructor's lecture. In order to facilitate student-driven investigation, the class is designed as discussion-based. Through frequent small group discussions, students have opportunities to learn from each other by sharing their ideas. Further, during the latter part of the term, students themselves become discussion leaders to reinforce inquiry-based learning. As discussion leaders, they generate reading questions and discussion slides for their classmates.

Teaching materials

- *Language and Society in Japan*, Nanette Gottlieb, 2005
- *Japanese Language, Gender, and Ideology: Cultural Models and Real People*, Shigeko Okamoto and Janet Shibamoto Smith (eds.), 2004

Class activities

The class generally starts with talking about students' responses to an assigned short exercise as a warm-up. The class then goes over the reading questions with small group discussions. Different activities are also incorporated for students to solidify their understandings of the issues. These activities often highlight the Japanese language content as shown below.

➢ Japanese Honorifics
This activity was utilized when the class discussed gender and politeness in Japanese. The central theme of the discussion was the stereotypical notion that women speak more politely than men in Japan. The Japanese honorifics play a vital role in showing politeness in Japan. However, the concept of honorifics might seem quite complex to many students without the Japanese language knowledge. Hence, the explanation was focused on *sonkee-go* (respectful words) and *kenjoo-go* (humble words). As Okamoto (2004) illustrates, *sonkee-go* are used to elevate the person to be respected, while *kenjoo-go* lower another person (usually the speaker) to show modesty.
The instructor explained the differences between *sonkee-go* and *kenjoo-go* using *taberu* (to eat) and *suru* (to do) as examples. *Taberu*'s *sonkee-go* form is *meshiagaru* (*meshiagarimasu* in a formal context)

and *kenjyoo-go* form is *itadaku* (*itadakimasu* in a formal context). Similarly, *suru* has *sonkee-go* and *kenjoo-go* forms, *nasaru* (*nasaimasu* in a formal context) and *itasu* (*itashimasu* in a formal context), respectively. Students then worked on a worksheet in small groups. In the first section of the worksheet, students filled in blanks by choosing an appropriate form from the table provided. They were advised to think about the context of the interaction when answering. Some examples are shown below.

Friend A: *Oishii yo.* _____ Friend B: *Un,* _____
It's delicious. Will you eat it? Yes, I'll eat it.

Boss: *Keeki, doozo.* Subordinate: *Arigatoo gozaimasu.* _____
Here it is. A cake. Thank you very much. I'll eat it.

Subordinate: *Keeki,* _____ *ka.* Boss: *Un, arigatoo.*
Would you eat the cake? Yes, thanks.

In the second section, they corrected underlined parts of the sentences using the options provided. The following is an example.

(to a friend) Projekuto wa itsu <u>nasaimasu</u> ka.
When will you do the project?

➢ Gender and First-Person Pronouns
This activity was designed to further students' understanding of individual linguistic choice and the portrayal of their identity through that choice. One of the salient Japanese linguistic features that index the speaker's gender is first-person pronouns. The class learned some stereotypical use of first-person pronouns in this activity, before discussing divergent uses by teenagers in Japan. In standard Japanese, women and men are expected to use different first-person pronouns. Women are supposed to use *watashi* or *atashi* as a plain form, though *watashi* is also reserved for formal use for men. Moreover, women do not have the deprecatory level of pronoun like men's *ore* (Ide cited in Miyazaki).
In this activity, after the introduction of first-person pronouns, the class watched some short clips of Japanese *anime* and drama. The clips were from *Doraemon*, *Crayon Shin-chan*, and *Hana Yori Dango*. While watching, the instructor paused the clips immediately after a first-person pronoun was uttered. Students had to identify which pronoun it was. In *Doraemon*, for instance, the clip was stopped after Nobita said "*boku* (first-person pronoun for men)" in "*Boku wa matsutake ga tabetai noni* (I want to eat

some matsutake mushrooms though)." Subsequently, the students discussed what kind of characteristics can be displayed through these speakers' choices of the pronouns.

> Sexist Language

This activity was created as a follow-up, after the class discussed the sexist language and changes in words in public discourse to eliminate such language use in Japan. The instructor introduced some examples of the words that are often used in contemporary Japan, where the social expectations toward genders are apparent. Those examples and their literal English meanings are *joshi ryoku* (girls' power), *megata kyojin* (female titans), *kotoba bijin* (language beauty), *bentoo danshi* (lunch box boys), and *iku men* (parenting men). The class first guessed what these words meant by the literal translations. The instructor then described them more in details.

- *Joshi ryoku.* It generally refers to the scale of women's attractiveness in a somewhat conventional sense, such as their household skills, gentle demeanors, and sophistication.
- *Megata kyojin.* This term was taken from Japanese *anime*, *Attack on Titan*. Despite the many male titans in that *anime*, the word "male" does not appear to describe them.
- *Kotoba bijin.* It usually suggests a woman who can handle the use of language beautifully.
- *Bentoo danshi.* They are men who make their own lunch box.
- *Iku men.* They refer to men who are spontaneous and enthusiastic toward parenting. The word *iku* came from *ikuji* (child rearing).

The class was then split into small groups. They discussed these words in comparison to the sexist words in the reading, the reasons why none of these words have the equivalent expressions to describe the opposite genders, and the possible cultural assumptions in these terms.

> Loanwords

One characteristic of loanwords in Japan is that they are written in *katakana* characters. Therefore, it is important for the students to have the basic knowledge of the Japanese writing system, *hiragana*, *katakana*, and *kanji* characters. The instructor first explained the differences between these characters in terms of their usages and shapes. They can be visually distinguishable. *Hiragana* generally has round and curved shape, whereas *katakana* is more straight and sharp. Even though *kanji*'s shapes vary, they tend to appear more complicated than *hiragana* and *katakana*.

Next, the students were divided into small groups. *Hiragana* characters were used for grouping. Specifically, each student picked a card with one *hiragana* character with a reading, for example, あ with "a," and found the classmates who had the same character to form a group. They then looked at a breakfast menu of a Japanese restaurant on the Internet and identified different characters' classifications together based on their shapes. In the menu, the majority of *katakana* appears in the names of Western style breakfast, such as *sukuranburu mooningu* (scrambled eggs breakfast). In contrast, *hiragana* and *kanji* are used mainly in the names of Japanese style breakfast as in *yakizakana no asateeshoku* (grilled fish breakfast).

➢ Girl-graphs

The class did this quick exercise, when they learned about adolescent Japanese girls' writing style called *gyaru-moji* or girl-graphs. Japanese adolescent girls use *gyaru-moji* as a group identity marking as well as a form of resistance to the parent culture (Miller). They are typically very hard to read with the uses of deconstructed characters, the math or science symbols, dismantled *kana* and *kanji* characters, etc. (Miller). In this activity, the students identified the characters of the words written in *gyaru-moji* style on a worksheet in small groups. The lists of *katakana* and *hiragana* characters were also provided so that they could match the characters in the words with the ones in the lists. A few examples from the worksheet are shown below.

オヤス彡 *oyasumi* (good night)
⊃〃めωナよ±あレゝ *gomennasai* (I'm sorry)
こωL=ちレ£ *konnichiwa* (hello)
レ卞"w(キ *genki* (how are you?)

Ideas for future class activities

The language component can be integrated even more in the future. For instance, in the discussion of first-person pronouns, students could learn a relatively simple grammatical structure "(choice of first-person pronoun) *wa* (name) *desu* (I am name)." When the class topic is the use of loanwords, they could find the *katakana* characters for their names and write them. They could also learn some formal and informal expressions like *ohayoo gozaimasu* and *ohayoo* (formal and informal of good morning) under the topic of politeness and use these expressions as greetings in every class afterward.

Furthermore, it might be relevant to incorporate more cultural elements besides sociolinguistics. For example, students are often curious about lesbian, gay, bisexual, transgender, queer (LGBTQ) issues in Japan after reading about gay male and female speech. It may be a good idea to have the class watch films with cultural components such as *Karera ga honki de amu toki wa* (*Close-Knit*) and discuss the themes afterward.

Evaluation

The evaluation was conducted through formative and summative assessments including class participation, exercises, leading class discussion, short papers, midterm examination, and a final paper. For the final paper, students were asked to analyze the perspectives studied in this course, using a text or visual media, a survey, or an interview. They could also write about a language other than Japanese and discuss the similarities and differences. Some of the topics they chose include lesbian speech in the United States, codeswitching and personal identity, and the use of *kanji* in Japan and South Korea. The rubric of the final paper consists of the following ten categories.

- Thesis (10%): Easily identifiable, plausible, sophisticated, and clear
- Content (10%): Balanced presentation of relevant and legitimate information
- Organization (10%): Information in clear sequence
- Logic and transition (10%): Logical flow of ideas with transitions.
- Development (10%): Specific and highly effective examples/evidence relating main and supporting points to each other
- Tone (10%): Professional and appropriate for an academic paper
- Sentence structure (10%): Well-phrased sentences with varied length and structure
- Grammar, spelling, and mechanics (10%): Should be free of errors
- References (10%): Sources are incorporated logically and insightfully
- Quality of references (10%): Primarily professional/scholarly journals or book chapters

Caveats and reflections

The strength of this course was being able to facilitate students' critical thinking about their own culture by exposing them to diverse topics in Japanese sociolinguistics, as they constantly interpreted the sociolinguistic phenomena of their own languages in comparison. The weakness is that some students with Japanese language background occasionally dominated the group discussions. In the future, this issue may be resolved by sometimes grouping students without language background together instead of the random grouping, especially when Japanese language content plays a central role in the activity. Offering this course is very beneficial for the students to be able to learn to think globally as well as locally as emphasized in our college's mission statement. Moreover, with the inclusion of Japanese language content, this course helps students realize that culture begins with language, which is in our departmental mission statement. Hence, it plays an important role in the overall mission of our department and college.

References

Ide, Sachiko. *Josee go no sekai (The World of Women's Language)*. Meiji Shoin, 1997.
Justice, Christopher, et al. "Inquiry in Higher Education: Reflections and Directions on Course Design and Teaching Methods." *Innovative Higher Education*, vol. 31, no. 4, 2007, pp. 201–214.
Miller, Laura. "Subversive Script and Novel Graphs in Japanese Girls' Culture." *Language and Communication*, vol. 31, no. 1, 2011, pp. 16–26.
Miyazaki, Ayumi. "Japanese Junior High School Girls' and Boys' First-Person Pronoun Use and Their Social World." *Japanese Language, Gender, and Ideology: Cultural Models and Real People*, edited by Shigeko Okamoto and Janet Shibamoto Smith. Oxford University Press, 2004, pp. 256–274.
Okamoto, Shigeko. "Ideology in Linguistic Practice and Analysis: Gender and Politeness in Japanese Revisited." *Japanese Language, Gender, and Ideology: Cultural Models and Real People*, edited by Shigeko Okamoto and Janet Shibamoto Smith. Oxford University Press, 2004, pp. 38–56.
Silverstein, Michael. "Language Structure and Linguistic Ideology." *The Elements: A Parasession on Linguistic Units and Levels*, edited by Paul R. Clyne, William F. Hanks, and Carol F. Hofbauer. Chicago Linguistic Society, 1979, pp. 193–247.

Teaching material references

Abe, Hiroko. "Queen's Speech and the Playful Plundering of Women's Language." *Queer Japanese: Gender and Sexual Identities through Linguistic Practices*, edited by Hiroko Abe. Palgrave Macmillan, 2010, pp. 97–134.
Gottlieb, Nanette. *Language and Society in Japan*. Cambridge University Press, 2005.
Inoue, Miyako. "Defamiliarizing Japanese Women's Language: Strategies and Tactics of Female Office Workers." *Vicarious Language: Gender and Linguistic Modernity in Japan*, edited by Miyako Inoue. University of California Press, 2006, pp. 252–277.

Iwasaki, Noriko. "Learning L2 Japanese 'Politeness' and 'Impoliteness': Young American Men's Dilemmas during Study Abroad." *Japanese Language and Literature*, vol. 45, no. 1, 2011, pp. 67–106.

Okamoto, Shigeko, and Janet Shibamoto Smith. *Japanese Language, Gender, and Ideology: Cultural Models and Real People*. Oxford University Press, 2004.

Sreetharan, Cindi. "Students, Sarariiman (pl.), and Seniors: Japanese Men's Use of 'Manly' Speech Register." *Language in Society*, vol. 33, no. 1, 2004, pp. 81–107.

Stanlaw, James. *Japanese English: Language and Culture Contact*. Hong Kong University Press, 2005.

Part III
Culture

11 Teaching *katakana* in a cool Japan culture course

Yumiko Tashiro

Course Title: EALL175 Cool Japan: A Visual Journey through Anime, Manga, Robots, Language and Culture
Course Level: Freshman or Sophomore
Language(s) in Focus: Japanese
Course Type: Japanese culture

Contextualization of topic

This is an introductory course that examines a variety of visual materials such as *manga*, *anime*, and unique social phenomena observable in Japan through reading materials, discussions, and hands-on experiences to understand Japanese culture and society. By being exposed to and analyzing different forms of Japanese traditional and contemporary culture, students deepen their understanding of the interaction between Japan's popular culture and Japanese society. They develop a multicultural and international perspective that will help them when encountering a culture other than their own. In order to avoid imposing stereotypical views, the diversity and fluidity of the cultures are emphasized by helping students realize that each individual belongs to multiple social groups, which may be contradictory and complex, as discussed by Atkinson and Kubota. Thus, the course includes assignments and discussions to describe the important aspects of their own cultures to show their membership of the culture by reflecting on their own experiences. Only one of the three writing systems, *katakana*, is taught in this course due to limited time, because it is mainly used to transcribe Western foreign words including English and onomatopoeia, which appear extensively in *manga*.

Course logistics

It is a 4-credit-hour course where the class meets four times each week; twice for 2-hour lectures and twice for 3-hour cultural and language workshops. There is no prerequisite to take this course. It provides credit for both the Cultural Core of East Asian Languages and Literature majors and for Humanities in the General Education curriculum.

Course objectives

The course objectives are as follows:

- To gain a general understanding of Japanese culture and customs of modern society in relation to visual materials and historical backgrounds
- To develop one's own perspectives by critically thinking of and analyzing both Japanese culture and one's own
- To understand history and structures of Japanese *manga/anime* and create an original digital short *manga* story as a group project
- To learn how to explore the latest cultural information by using online resources

Learning outcomes

Students completing this course will be able to

- Describe Japanese perspectives about robots, technology, language, religion, food, and gender roles by comparing their own perspectives with some examples reflecting historical backgrounds
- Demonstrate distinctive features of Japanese *manga* by comparing to American and other countries' comics
- Read *katakana* letters and meaningful words, and write their own names in *katakana*
- Make a digital *manga* that reflects the characteristics of *manga* such as effectively using English or original onomatopoeia and designing images
- Search and obtain necessary and appropriate information using online resources to do academic research on popular culture

Curricular structure

Students present and exchange their ideas and opinions in discussions in class. They also make an informative presentation on Japanese cultural items of their choice (e.g., pet robots, maid café, Harajuku fashion) and lead a class discussion in groups formed by topics of interest. Most of them expand on the same topic as they had chosen for cultural items presentation when writing their research paper. Hands-on experiences, which are encouraged in the short-term intensive courses, also provide invaluable opportunities for the students. Cultural lab reports are submitted after each cultural lab to provide detailed description of their experience. The first report, however, is on their own culture. The following is the composition of each student's grades.

(20%) Attendance and Participation
(10%) Group Presentation on Japanese cultural items
(10%) Language Quizzes (*Katakana*/Vocabulary)
(20%) Cultural Lab Reports (500 words minimum × 4)
(10%) Digital Comic Project
(30%) One research paper (2000 words minimum)

Theoretical framework

The course is based on thematic units. The syllabus is built on the key concepts described in its main textbook *Japanese Popular Culture and Globalization* by Tsutsui. In his book, Tsutsui points out four central themes of Japanese popular culture: an apocalyptic imagination, fascination with the monstrous, a soft spot for the cute, and mecha fantasies. The textbook was adopted because it provides an academic framework for exploring Japanese popular culture, a subject which might have been of personal interest since childhood. Several pieces of *manga* and films were selected based on Tsutsui's concepts determined by the accessibility of the materials. In order to understand the history of *manga* and a variety of its genres, the works on gourmet and for girls were added to the list. Multiple topics that could attract students' interest were chosen so that they would be able to discern the culture through the four themes. The topics covered in this course are robots/technology, food, fashion, religion, gender roles, and racial diversity. Each topic is introduced through *manga* or films, in addition to its related book chapters and academic articles.

Teaching materials

- *Japanese Popular Culture and Globalization*, William Tsutsui, 2010
- *Kodansha's Katakana Workbook*, Anne Matsumoto Stewart, 2012
- *Astro Boy*, Osamu Tezuka, 2002

A complete list of the teaching materials is provided in the References section at the end of this chapter.

Class activities

The course content delivery adopts two formats: classroom or language lab lectures and cultural workshops. Lectures last approximately 20–30 min. and are followed by class discussion or language practice. The activities provided in the cultural workshops include Asian brush painting, character *bento* (lunchbox) making, and Japanese tea ceremony. Details of the language lab activities are provided below.

➤ Learning *Katakana*
 The history of the Japanese writing system illustrates that Japan has been greatly influenced by Chinese and Western languages. Two types of scripts, both *hiragana* and *katakana* were derived from visually intricate Chinese characters (*kanji*). As *katakana* is mainly used to transcribe Western loanwords, and the loanwords written in *katakana* (e.g., レストラン for restaurant) consist of around 10% of Japanese vocabulary (Matsushita), the ability to recognize *katakana* letters is helpful in learning Japanese. In this course, the writing system of Japanese is introduced and then each *katakana* letter is shown with a sound representation, the way of writing letters with stroke order, and mnemonics using an image. A set of 46 *katakana* letters are introduced in a series of three classes: 23 letters in the first and second sessions, special sounds including voiced and semi-voiced consonants and contracted sounds in the third session. Three recognition quizzes are given in the following *katakana* session, which are usually one week after new letters are introduced. They are only required to write their own name in *katakana*. The time allocated is as follows: the first 50-min. session for learning the writing system and the first set of 23 letters, the second session for the second set of letters and onomatopoeia, and the third session for the special sounds, practicing their names, and *katakana* vocabulary.

➤ Learning *Katakana* Vocabulary
 The adaptation of foreign words into Japanese language is linked to the modification of foreign materials in Japanese culture, for example, the influence of American cartoons to the prosperity of Japanese animation. After the history of loanwords in Japanese is introduced, the students discuss how loanwords were adopted in English and other languages and how *katakana* words are perceived by native speakers of Japanese by examining some packages of commercial products whose brand names and product descriptions are written in *katakana* (Stanlaw), for example, a gummy

candy package uses ジューシー (juicy) and ソフト (soft). The students observed that the original meanings of the foreign words are frequently limited or modified in the process of adaptation.

> Learning Onomatopoeia (50 min.)
Onomatopoeia is generally a word that imitates the natural sound of a thing, but Japanese onomatopoeia includes numerous mimetic words that refer to an action or condition that does not involve any sound. They are used often in various contexts, such as in daily conversations and sound effects in comics. This activity is based on a lesson plan for a Japanese class for elementary students in Japan (www.waseda.jp/prj-tagengo2013/blog/html/_downloads/1-3.pdf). The students first compare onomatopoeia in different languages pertaining to animal sounds and the action of walking and identify distinctive characteristics depending on languages. Japanese TV commercials are also used to demonstrate how effectively onomatopoeia could convey messages to promote products. Then, the students work in small groups to create new onomatopoeias that express various sounds made by different flat sheet materials, for example, copy paper, aluminum foil, tissue paper, and a paper towel. They are required to incorporate multiple onomatopoeias in their digital *manga* story as well.

> Making Emoji (50 min. lecture on *kanji* and emoji history)
Emoji, invented by Japanese interface designer Shigetaka Kurita, is one of the topics covered in the language labs in connection with the topic of technology. Chinese characters are not sound-based, but meaning-based, unlike English and other major European languages using the Roman alphabet. This emoji activity is conducted after the writing system of Japanese is introduced. The instructor displays several basic Chinese characters that clearly illustrate the examples of pictograms and ideograms, whose concepts have been adapted as emoji. The students have been familiar with mobile phones and computers for most of their lives and can be a user of emoji without realizing its origin. They individually create a new emoji that would be useful if it existed on a website designed for that purpose (https://www.pizap.com/pizap-app.php?initialstate=emoji). Figure 11.1 is a sample of my student's work and the emoji indicates a situation in which a person cannot make oneself understood to the listener. After creating an original emoji in class, they presented it to each other in small groups by sharing its meaning, usage, and design they would like to appeal. This activity helps them appreciate the concept of *kanji* representation as well as the connection between the language and technology.

Figure 11.1 Emoji Created by Student.
Image Provided by Yumiko Tashiro.

> Making a Digital *Manga* Story
> Using an iOS app called "Comic Life 3 (http://plasq.com/apps/comiclife/ios/)," students pairs create a four- or six-page *manga* story. They choose one scene to illustrate their college life, supposing they will present it to prospective high school students. With the help of an IT technologist on campus, a session on how to use the app is arranged (30 min.). Before the tech session, they discussed their campus culture such as unique campus events and school tradition, then they picked their topic so that no pair would choose the same one (20 min.). One of the advantages of the app is taking and installing photos in a single device and not needing to draw pictures unless they so desired. They are also told to use their own photos to solve copyright issues. The app is available for Microsoft Windows (http://plasq.com/

Teaching katakana in Japan culture course   121

Figure 11.2 Sample Pages from a Student *Manga* Project.
Image Provided by Yumiko Tashiro.

apps/comiclife/macwin/), but the course used iPads because the IT service offered iPad loan. Preparation for the use of onomatopoeia, such as size, font style, and where it should be placed in a frame or page, is discussed during the session on onomatopoeia. Students' work is later combined in a PDF file and shared electronically among the students.

Ideas for future class activities

Students suggested focusing on *manga* subgenres such as *manga* for girls and boys as the subject of the assignment for student creative work. If a similar course is offered during a regular semester, students could work on their creations longer and revise multiple times by receiving feedback from both their instructor and classmates.

Evaluation

The grade directly relating to the topic of the language was the *katakana* vocabulary quizzes. These are assigned to encourage them to memorize the association between sound representation and written letters. In the *manga* project, a summative assessment was only given after the submission due to time constraints. The rubric components include agreement between topic and storyline, free from copyright, effective use of onomatopoeia, and *manga* formatting.

Student feedback

According to the course evaluation, it was well received. Students considered the strengths of this course as variety of the subjects, multiple culture workshops, and various creative activities. Thus, the course successfully embraced the content to which every student could relate. Many of them did not think learning *katakana* was difficult probably because it was a fairly straightforward assignment. However, there was a comment saying that it was difficult balancing the language and cultural aspects of the course.

Caveats and reflections

It is undeniable that students enjoyed cultural workshops more than learning *katakana*, although they were actively engaged in creating emoji and onomatopoeia in the language labs. As their primary purpose of taking such a culture course is not to learn the language, they might not be interested in taking language courses. The course, however, attracted students from different fields and demonstrated that there was a group of students with an interest in Japanese culture. The students who took this course had studied at least one foreign language before and most of them had studied European languages. Their language learning experience and knowledge was useful enough to analyze a new language even in such limited subjects. In this sense, this course was able to expose students to language and culture that could have been less accessible for them.

In order to promote language courses, a culture course might be better offered during a regular academic semester, encouraging students in the culture course to take a language course at the same time. Then, the contents covered in a language section in the culture course could add a different theme by eliminating tasks requiring rote memorization. It could also make it possible for the language and culture course to compensate for each other in terms of content. It is not an easy task to increase the enrollment of the language courses in a short time, but this course provided access to students with different backgrounds who may not otherwise take language courses. Although the instructor experienced anxiety at times over the issue of expertise, offering this course helps the language program become more visible on campus. Regardless of the course type, it is necessary and meaningful to provide interactive cultural activities as often as possible to foster students' understanding of the cultural diversity on campus.

References

Atkinson, Dwight. "TESOL and Culture." *TESOL Quarterly*, vol. 33, no. 4, 1999, pp. 625–654.
Kubota, Ryuko. "Critical Teaching of Japanese Culture." *Japanese Language and Literature*, vol. 37, 2003, pp. 67–87.
———. "Nihongo kyoiku ni okeru bunka [Culture in Japanese Language Education]." *America ni okeru nihongo kyoiku [Japanese Language Education in the United States]*, edited by Yasuhiko Tohsaku, 2014. PDF.
Matsushita, Tatsuhiko. *Nihongo wo yomu tameno goi database (Kyoushi-you) [Japanese Academic Word Data from the Vocabulary Database for Reading Japanese (VDRJ) for Teachers]* Ver. *1.01*, 2011.
Stanlaw, James. "Is It *naisu* Rice or Good *gohan*?: In Japan, It's Not What You Eat, but How You Say It." *Japanese English: Language and Culture Contact*. Hong Kong University Press, 2004, pp. 189–210.

Teaching material references

Clarke, Hugh. "Language." *The Cambridge Companion to Modern Japanese Culture*, edited by Yoshio Sugimoto, Cambridge University Press, 2009, pp. 56–75.
Fukuda, Hiroko. "Introduction: An Overview of Onomatopoeia." *Jazz Up Your Japanese with Onomatopoeia: For All Levels*, Kodansha USA, 2003, pp. 8–36.
Mizuno, Ryotaro. "Feelings & Emotions." *Onomato Perapera: An Illustrated Guide to Japanese Onomatopoeia*, Tokyodo Shuppan, 2014, pp. 79–99.
Stewart, Anne Matsumoto. *Kodansha's Katakana Workbook*. Kodansha USA, 2012.
Tezuka, Osamu. *Astro Boy Volume 3*. Dark Horse Comics, 2002.
Tsutsui, William M. *Japanese Popular Culture and Globalization*. Association for Asian Studies, 2010.

12 Understanding Chinese behavioral culture through cross-cultural communication

Junqing (Jessie) Jia

Course Title: Chinese 165: Americans and Chinese: Case Studies of Cross-cultural Communication
Course Level: Freshman
Language(s) in Focus: Chinese
Course Type: Chinese Culture, Cross-cultural Communication

Contextualization of topic

Truly learning a foreign language is more than just the simple command of words or phrases. Behavioral culture is a significant aspect of foreign language education, especially when the target culture is largely distinct from one's base culture. Through selected texts, film screenings, role-play, and skit performances, students learn to identify and ethnographically analyze differences in the behavioral culture between Americans and Chinese. They are also led to explore these behavioral differences from an interdisciplinary humanities perspective that involves knowledge of Chinese language, history, literature, and performance studies.

Course logistics

This is a 1-credit-hour course that meets face-to-face, twice per week (Tuesday and Thursday), with each session lasting 75 min. This is an introductory culture course with no prerequisite. Chinese majors are required to take at least one culture course at my institution. It is highly recommended that students who have plans to study abroad take at least one culture course before embarking on study in China.

Course objectives

- Understanding cross-cultural diversity and learning complex cultural behaviors through class discussions and presentations
- Developing a discourse that facilitates communication and expression about how cultural behaviors are understood and learned
- Developing learning curiosity and research interest in foreign languages and cultural studies

Learning outcomes

Students are expected to

- Demonstrate better understanding of cross-cultural diversity and interact more effectively with their counterparts from different cultures
- Improve their critical thinking skills through conducting cross-cultural observations and analysis
- Use materials related to Chinese and American culture to improve their oral and written cross-cultural communication skills

Curricular structure

Twelve topics are explored throughout the semester including Chinese "face" culture, parenting, social classes, networking, the art of gift giving, and language use in various contexts. Each week is designed as a learning circle with one assigned topic. Although both classes on Tuesday and Thursday are lecture and discussion-based, Tuesday's classes are reading and video based while Thursday's classes focus on learners' observation and analysis.

Students are evaluated based on the following criteria:

(15%) Attendance

(40%) Class participation. Students are expected to read the assigned materials before each class and participate in class discussions, mini presentations, and performance sessions.

(15%) Midterm reflection paper. Students are required to critically illustrate their understanding of one of the discussed topics.

(30%) Final individual project. This summative assessment encourages students to communicate with native speakers of Chinese and examines how students analyze cross-cultural interactions through a diverse and critical lens.

Theoretical framework

One fundamental goal of the course is to deepen students' understanding of cultural complexity and improve their critical and analytical competences in cross-cultural communication. The backward design approach was adopted to identify the course objectives discussed above. The course is mostly built upon these three pedagogical frameworks: First, the model of experiential learning process (Kolb 21) that consists of four cyclic stages:

- Concrete experiences
- Observations and reflection
- Formation of abstract concepts and generalization
- Testing implications of concepts in new situations

Based on this model, students are encouraged to regularly participate, observe, and reflect on concrete cross-cultural experiences. They discuss their assumptions during the class and test the implications through designed classroom activities or activities outside of the classroom.

Second, alongside scholars who understand foreign language learning as accumulating memories of doing things in the target language (Walker and Noda 197), I consider behavioral culture as both the agent and target of learning in this course. For example, the term of "face" (*mianzi*) is a key concept when introducing Chinese culture to Westerners. However, instead of focusing on introducing what "face" is, this course guides students to explore how people gain "face" through doing certain things and what behaviors to avoid to prevent losing "face." As a result, students not only establish competences of communicating in different cultures, they also learn to behave in ways that are culturally appropriate. For students who already know Chinese language, the course provides them an opportunity to reflect their linguistic and cultural knowledge in contextualized cases. Students with no previous background of learning Chinese or other foreign languages are equipped with an observant and analytical learning mechanism that contributes to their long-term development.

Third, the course design is influenced by Dörnyei and his colleagues' "L2 Motivational Self System." Muir and Dörnyei define vision as "the mental representation of the sensory experience of a future goal state" (357), which should be used for pedagogical design to create effective motivational pathways. In other words, to motivate a student to learn a foreign language, we can begin with creating a vision of themselves successfully participating in the target culture. Although the course is conducted in English, students are highly encouraged to mimic Chinese cultural behaviors and learn simple Chinese words when acting out skits. The memories they have established through these class activities could serve as the vision of themselves, which could potentially motivate them to learn more about the language and culture.

In addition to being built using three pedagogical frameworks, this course is thematically organized for two reasons. First, it is unrealistic to conduct a comprehensive survey of cross-cultural communication within the term of one semester. Selecting 10–12 specific topics helps both the instructor and students to organize the contents and realize the progress. Second, as discussed, students are expected to observe and visualize concrete real-world experiences. Without specified themes and performance, students are not able to identify the cases and establish the effective "motivational self."

Teaching materials

- *Americans & Chinese: Passage to Differences*, Francis Hsu, 1981
- *Eat Shandong: From Personal Experience to a Pedagogy of a Second Culture*, Eric Shepherd, 2005

Additional course materials are listed in the References section.

Class activities

Each week one pre-selected topic is introduced over two sessions for a total of 150 min. of class time. On Tuesday, the instructor introduces the key concepts (15 min.) and leads an interactive group discussion (60 min.). Students are expected to prepare comments and questions in advance. Each Thursday class is a continuation of Tuesday's topic that begins with each student sharing a 3–5-min. mini presentation on any aspect of the topic (20 min.). Students are required to take notes on their classmates' mini presentation and raise questions (5 min.). Following the mini presentation, the instructor resumes the discussions of Tuesday's class (20 min.). Students then identify and conclude topic-related cultural rules (15 min.) and perform accordingly (15 min.). Using one of the topics, "Banquet and Face," as the example, the following class activities are adopted to achieve the course objectives:

➢ Introducing the key concepts in both English and Chinese, and discussing the definitions (15–20 min.)

The instructor prepares 20–25 PowerPoint slides for each topic. Two to three slides are designed to introduce key terms. For example, some major terms for the above topic include face (*mianzi*), connections (*guanxi*), and feelings (*ganqing*). At the beginning of Tuesday's class, students discuss how these three concepts are defined in both cultures by addressing the reading materials and using concrete examples. Considering the culture-specific characteristics of these terms, students are also strongly encouraged to be familiar with the Chinese meanings and pronunciation of these words. The purpose of this activity is to help students gain familiarity with the terms and establish a discourse to discuss the topic.

➢ Using the prepared PowerPoint slides to conduct lectures and discussions

Instructor-led lectures play a major role for each Tuesday session (50–60 min.). Although the instructor leads the class to review the assigned materials, the PowerPoint slides also include an adequate amount of discussion questions to engage students. Some questions are content-based while others are open-ended and require students to form their own opinions.

➢ Thursday's class always begins with a themed mini presentation session (20–25 min.)

Students share their experiences and observations of cultural behaviors. For example, during the week of "Banquet and Face," the mini presentation was titled "Face and My Social Skills." Students narrate in detail how they participated in social events such as banquets or conferences. They are also encouraged to perform a part of the discussed event so that the classmates can visualize and analyze the cultural behaviors. Students who know Chinese are encouraged to introduce ritual expressions related to those contexts. For instance, Chinese people bow and say *qingduozhijiao* when exchanging business cards or contact information. The literal translation of the phrase is "please advise (me) often," which does not make sense to the native English speakers. Therefore, when students introduce these types of phrases in their mini presentation, the instructor writes the expressions in Romanized Chinese and English on the blackboard. One thing to note is that having students introduce some language knowledge to their classmates can be particularly rewarding but the instructor should not spend too much time explaining Chinese grammar or correcting student's pronunciations.

➢ Group work where students identify "cultural rules" from specific contexts (15–20 min.)
This activity is conducted during Thursday's class after students are relatively familiar with the assigned materials. The purpose of this activity is to help students review the topic and form their revised hypothesis. For example, when discussing Chinese banquet etiquette, students need to determine what roles different people play, how hosts and guests behave differently and how foreigners are positioned in this type of social event. By the end of this activity, each group needs to write their summarized rules on the blackboard.
➢ Using the "cultural rules" summarized during group work along with additions from the instructor, students design and act out a skit (15–20 min.)
Although students perform in English, they need to adopt appropriate Chinese cultural behaviors. As a result, students show a particularly high level of participation in learning and performing the Chinese expressions in the provided contexts.

Ideas for future class activities

Considering the growing number of international students from China on campus, it would be ideal to recruit some of those students to take the course, thus allowing more authentic cross-cultural communication activities to be designed. For example, students with different cultural background can form a team and compose a booklet on "How to behave on a Chinese/American campus." Students who know Chinese language should also be encouraged to introduce some simple but useful Chinese ritual expressions or college slang to the class.

Evaluation

Question-led discussion, mini presentations, and the performance session are considered as formative assessment in the learning process where the instructor obtain an idea of how well students understand the course materials and how involved they are with the classroom activities. In addition, students are required to write a five-page midterm reflection paper to illustrate their understanding of one or more discussed topics. The paper is expected to be constructed upon readings, online materials as well as their own experience in cross-cultural communication. By the end of the semester, as a summative assessment, students are required to compose a final paper on one of the 12 topics that have been discussed in the class such as "face" culture, the art of gift giving, and Chinese language use in various contexts. Students are also required to include a report on interviews with at least three people with cross-cultural experiences on the selected topic. They are highly encouraged to use their own or classmates' mini presentations to establish their arguments. They also give an 8–10-min. presentation on their final paper two weeks before the final draft is due.

Table 12.1 shows the rubric that is used to evaluate the final project.

Table 12.1 Final Project Rubric

Final presentation (30%)	• Main argument is clear and interesting.
	• The presentation utilizes assigned and additional learning materials.
	• The presentations provide persuasive and concrete examples.
	• The presenter answers questions well.
Definition/concept understanding (15%)	• The paper indicates a good understanding of discussed key terms.
	• The paper defines at least three key concepts in both Chinese and American cultures.
Arguments (15%)	• Paper provides evidence to support the arguments.
	• Paper uses assigned and additional sources appropriately.
Interviews (15%)	• Student interview at least three people with cross-culture experiences.
	• The interviews support or challenge the arguments.
	• Different opinions were described clearly and convincingly.
Structure/organization (10%)	• Clearly illustrate the main arguments.
	• Flow clearly from section to section.
	• Reader friendly. Strong opening and conclusion.
Supports/examples (10%)	• Paper addresses materials from small-talk session.
	• Supports and examples strengthen the arguments.
Format/citation /usage (5%)	• Abstract, citation, references, grammar, spelling, overall clarity.

Student feedback

Students indicated that the course gave them a deeper understanding of Chinese language and cultural behaviors. Students with prior Chinese language course experience commented that they gained a new appreciation for the importance of culture in their Chinese studies.

Caveats and reflections

The goal of my department is to introduce students to the region's changing identity while emphasizing language proficiency. Most students who took the course indicated a strong interest in further exploring Chinese language and culture. They have achieved a solid understanding that different cultures shape people's behaviors and it takes extensive observation, adaptation, and communication for one to perform in a foreign language. They have also successfully established positive memories of using a foreign language to interact with others from class activities. These strengths of this course align with the college's goal of developing global citizens who can critically engage with multiple cultural traditions and perspectives. One area of improvement for the course would be to provide real-life learning opportunities that allow students to observe how Chinese people behave in authentic situations. To further enhance the effectiveness of the previously discussed classroom activities, students should be encouraged to engage with an authentic Chinese community.

References

Dörnyei, Zoltán. "The L2 Motivational Self System." *Motivation, Language Identity and the L2 Self*, edited by Zoltan Dörnyei and Ema Ushioda, Multilingual Matters, 2009, pp. 9–42.

Kolb, David. *Experiential Learning: Experience as the Source of Learning and Development*. Prentice Hall, 1984.

Muir, Christine, and Zoltán Dörnyei. "Directed Motivational Currents: Using Vision to Create Effective Motivational Pathways." *Studies in Second Language Learning and Teaching*, vol. 3, no. 3, 2013, pp. 357–375.

Walker, Galal, and Mari Noda. "Remembering the Future: Compiling Knowledge of Another Culture." *Reflecting on the Past to Shape the Future*, edited by Diane Birckbichler and Robert Terry, National Textbook Company, 2000, pp. 187–212.

Teaching material references

Gifted. Directed by Marc Webb. 20th Century Fox Home Entertainment, 2017.
Hsu, Francis. *Americans and Chinese: Passage to Differences.* 3rd ed., University Press of Hawaii, 1981.
The Karate Kid. Directed by Harald Zwart. Sony Pictures Home Entertainment, 2010.
McAloon, Patrick. *Studying in China: A Practical Handbook for Students: Take an Extraordinary Educational Trip to China.* Tuttle Publishing, 2014.
Shepherd, Eric. *Eat Shandong: From Personal Experience to a Pedagogy of a Second Culture.* National East Asian Languages Resource Center, Ohio State University, 2005.
Tiger, Caroline. *How to Behave: A Guide to Modern Manners.* Quirk Books, 2011.
Walker, Galal. *The Pedagogy of Performing Another Culture: Ti Yan Wen Hua Jiao Xue Fa.* National East Asian Languages Resource Center, Ohio State University, 2010.
Yang, Mayfair Mei-Hui. *Gifts, Favors, and Banquets: The Art of Social Relationships in China.* Cornell University Press, 2016.
Zhang, Ting, and Roger Stough. *Entrepreneurship and Economic Growth in China.* World Scientific, 2013.

13 Introducing the Portuguese language through Brazilian popular culture

Soraya Calheiros Nogueira

Course Title: HUM 3070 Brazilian Popular Culture
Course Level: Upper-Division
Language(s) in Focus: Portuguese
Course Type: Humanities, Culture

Contextualization of topic

Brazilian Popular Culture, HUM 3070, is designed to provide students with knowledge and understanding of popular culture in Brazil in its socioeconomic, political, and cultural context, while at the same time exposing them to Portuguese language. Throughout the semester, students learn Portuguese words and sentences that cannot be literally translated into English. The course introduces students to aspects of Brazilian culture such as Carnival, futebol, Capoeira, and Brazilian popular music, which are internationally known.

Course logistics

This is a 3-credit-hour course offered twice a week for 85 min., with no prerequisites. It is an elective course, created to support the interdisciplinary Portuguese Studies minor.

Course objectives

The course aims to

- Provide the necessary context, critical analysis of different theories, and perspectives on contemporary culture studies to prepare students for a better understanding of popular culture in Brazil

- Expose students to the Portuguese language in a cultural context
- Create pathways where students can make a valuable connection between a cultural context, language learning, and other disciplines
- Promote critical thinking and cultural awareness

Learning outcomes

Students will be able to

- Think critically about Brazilian popular culture through reflective writing exercises and class discussions
- Recognize and understand the meaning of some Portuguese words and sentences in a cultural context
- Connect the content of this course with other disciplines

Curricular structure

The curricular structure of this course, Brazilian Popular Culture, is interdisciplinary in nature. It combines language learning with other disciplines such as anthropology, sociology, political science, and history.

Throughout the semester, students are evaluated according to the following criteria:

(25%) Reading and Homework: Students receive handouts (writing prompts, keywords, and/or reading guides) that highlight vocabulary items to be mastered.
(35%) Exams: There are three essay exams during the semester. For example: Write an essay about the *Orixás*, including the following topics: the meaning and examples of *Orixás*, the difference between *Candomblé* and *Umbanda*, the influence of Africans on Brazilian society, examples of different *oferendas*, censorship, and African religion in Brazil.
(10%) Oral Presentation: This grade is based on the oral presentation of the topic the student has chosen for the final paper.
(10%) Class Participation: This grade is based on attendance.
(20%) Final Paper: This final project is about any topic on Brazilian culture connected to a different discipline (political science, anthropology, sociology, history, etc.) It must incorporate at least five different Portuguese terms.

Theoretical framework

The pedagogical framework employed is theme-based instruction that highlights the relationship of knowledge across academic disciplines. During the semester, six different topics are covered in the class: Introducing Brazil, The Orixás, Soccer Madness, Carnival, Brazilian Popular Music, and the visual art of Vik Muniz. For each of these topics, students are introduced to Portuguese terms. The course further employs an integrated curriculum approach. According to Shoemaker, an integrated curriculum emphasizes

> ...education that is organized in such a way that it cuts across subject-matter lines, bringing together various aspects of the curriculum into meaningful association to focus upon broad areas of study. It views learning and teaching in a holistic way and reflects the real world, which is interactive. (5)

Throughout the semester, students learn Portuguese words and sentences through the lens of an anthropologist, Roberto DaMatta, a sociologist, Gilberto Freyre, a historian, Marshal Eakin, and a law professor, Joseph A. Page. This interplay among disciplines allows students to make connections across courses, creating an opportunity for them to apply skills and knowledge learned in one class to those gained in a different one.

Teaching materials

Book

- *The Brazilians*, Joseph A. Page, 1995

DVD

- *Brazil Revealed*, Graham Booth, 2006
- *Favela Rising*, Jeff Zimbalist and Matt Mochary, 2010
- *Waste Land*, Lucy Walker, 2010

YouTube videos

- *Brasil, Brasil: Samba to Bossa Nova*, 2011
- *Brasil, Brasil: Tropicalia Revolution*, 2013
- *Brasil, Brasil: A Tale of Four Cities*, 2016
- *Capoeira, The Dance of Freedom*, 2013
- *Miracle Man: John of God*, 2016

- *Gods of Brazil*—Festour, 2013
- *Wide Angle*—Brazil in Black and White, 2013
- *Inside Rio Carnaval (2007)*, 2012
- *Lineker in Brazil: The Beautiful Game*, 2016
- *Kaapor Indians*—Brazil Amazon, 2010

Class activities

A typical lesson plan for the course includes the following:

- (5 min.) Attendance and homework check
- (15 min.) Discussion of a prompt about the reading of the day. Students work in pairs or groups of three, while the instructor monitors groups, answering possible questions
- (20 min.) Open class discussion: The instructor introduces the correct pronunciation of some Portuguese terms in a cultural context
- (20 min.) Students watch a video related to the class content
- (20 min.) Open class discussion: Students discuss connections between the video, information in the textbook, instructor's input, and other disciplines
- (5 min.) Assignment for the next class and final thoughts

Before class, student readings include chapters from *The Brazilians*, where they find several different Portuguese words. I provide them with a prompt to facilitate their reading at home and students write a paragraph for each topic, where they reflect on the meaning of the Portuguese words in a cultural context. In class, we work on meaning, pronunciation, and listening comprehension of the Portuguese terms.

In the chapter, Orixás, for example, I give students the following writing prompt:

- Who are *Ogum, Exu* and *Iemanjá, Preto Velho, malandro, caboclos, mãe de santo, pai de* santo, and *filho de santo*?
- Discuss the influence of African Religion on Brazil's culture: *Candomblé, Macumba, Xangô,* and *Umbanda*. Students should be able to establish a difference between these terms.
- What are *terreiros* and *Centro Espíritas*?
- Provide examples of religious syncretism. São Jorge and Nossa Senhora are associated with which entities in the African religion?
- Describe the initial phase of most ceremonies, the opening ritual and the focal event. Identify some Portuguese words and sentences from the ceremonies.

Introducing the Portuguese language 137

- Describe one of *Candomblés* major feast.
- Describe the dish *feijoada* and the history behind this national dish of Brazil.
- Describe *Capoeira* and the history behind this Brazilian martial arts.
- Explain the relationship between dictatorship, *censura*, and religion.
- Make connections between the content of this chapter with other disciplines.

After a group discussion of these topics, students watch the video *Gods of Brazil—Festour*. Several Portuguese words used in the reading and in class discussion are contextualized and reinforced by the video, which is narrated in English, with interviews in Portuguese with English subtitles. Students are exposed once more to the Portuguese phonetic structures and are able to recognize the words discussed in class.

From the reading, discussions, and videos, students learn, among other things, that *Ogum, Exu, Iemanjá*, and *Preto Velho* are the names of some African gods and goddesses that were incorporated into Brazilian Portuguese. They learn that *Candomblé, Umbanda, Xangô*, and *Macumba* are the names of different religions in Brazil. The national dish, *Feijoada*, was created by the enslaved people from Africa who cooked black beans with pork, and comes from the word *feijão* (beans) in Portuguese. *Terreiros* and *Centro Espíritas* are the names of their worship temples. They also learn about different accent marks used in some of these words and how they influence the Brazilian Portuguese pronunciation. For pronunciation purposes, I ask the students to repeat the Portuguese vocabulary list after me. Furthermore, I demonstrate the phonetic differences between Brazilian Portuguese and Portuguese from Portugal for all the terms used in class and ask the students to repeat them after me.

I ask the students to write down the terms they recognize from the video. Through this specific exercise, students will be able to practice three different language skills: pronunciation, listening comprehension, and writing.

For Brazilian popular music, I use a different format. Students do not read any information at home, since the topic is not covered by *The Brazilians*. I provide a vocabulary list of Portuguese terms to identify, pronounce, and define, based on a three-part documentary that is narrated in English, with several interviews in Portuguese with English subtitles.

Students construct the meaning of the Portuguese words and establish connections between some of the terms provided in the vocabulary list below (this list is for part I of the documentary *Brasil, Brasil: from Samba to Bossa Nova*).

- *Bahia & Samba*
- The enslaved people *& Samba*
- *Modinha*
- *Tia Ciata*
- *Donga—Pelo telefone*
- *Samba & Candomblé*
- *Chula*
- *choro*
- *Pixinguinha*
- *Malandro & samba*
- *Getúlio Vargas*
- *Dorival Cayme*
- *Carmen Miranda*
- *Recife-forró-Luiz Gonzaga—1940*
- *Bossa Nova*
- *João Gilberto, Tom Jobim & Vinícius de Moraes*
- *1962—Garota de Ipanema*
- *Jazz & Bossa Nova*

After watching the video, we come together as a class to go over the vocabulary to make sure they understand the meaning of the words and differences in pronunciation among speakers of Portuguese. Again, three language skills are emphasized: listening comprehension, writing, and speaking.

Ideas for future class activities

In the future, I will include an e-portfolio and Quizlet in this course. For each topic developed in class, I will ask the students to write the Portuguese terms in their e-portfolio. Furthermore, I will use Quizlet games in class to check students' comprehension of the meaning of Portuguese words. By the end of the semester, they should have a substantial list of contextualized Portuguese vocabulary. As a final activity, I will ask students to come to class with 10 different Portuguese words or sentences. I will ask them to sit in groups of three or four to discuss the nuances of these Portuguese terms. An e-portfolio and Quizlet games will enhance the learning process and provide an opportunity for students to reflect upon their progress in this class and others.

Evaluation

There are two forms of assignments in this class: formative (readings, writing, and participation) and summative (exams and essays). For exams, oral presentation, and final project, I use the following rubric:

Structure

- Introduction
- Development
- Conclusion

Content

- Connections across disciplines
- Correct use of Portuguese terms (spelling and meaning)
- Application of skills and theories learned in class

For the Final Project only, format is considered, including elements such as page length, line spacing, font, and the use of at least two bibliographic sources. Students are encouraged to write about a topic that overlaps in content with any other class they have taken or are currently taking.

Examples of student topics include

- Censorship in Brazil compared to censorship in Argentina (studied in this course and in history and political science as well)
- An indigenous tribe in Brazil and the environmental problems they currently are facing (connecting the content of this course to an anthropology course)
- *Bumba-meu-Boi*, a celebration typical from the north of Brazil (connecting the student's Ethnographic Field School study abroad experience to this course)

Caveats and reflections

Studying another language and culture can provide students with opportunities to learn and understand other voices and to open themselves to an appreciation of human diversity and cultural awareness around the globe. One of the strengths of the Brazilian Popular Culture course is that it promotes students' curiosity across disciplines. It also provides a deeper understanding of course content through connections to courses in other disciplines, while exposing students to the Portuguese language. By the end of this class, students will have learned how an anthropologist, a historian, a sociologist, a law professor, and a language instructor view the popular culture in Brazil. Furthermore, students will have learned more than 100 words and sentences in Portuguese, which can be a motivation to take a Portuguese language course in the future. However, a lack of a service-based learning experience—students learning from involvement in community service, internship programs, and other social welfare programs—is one of the weaknesses of this course. One of the goals of the integrated approach is not only to make a clear connection among various subjects but provide the learners with an opportunity to apply their knowledge in real life. This is a missing piece of this class. With the growing population of Brazilians in the state of Tennessee, it is something that could be incorporated in the near future.

As we prepare our students for the challenges of the 21st century, we should take into consideration the constant change of social, cultural, and economic contexts. It is our responsibility to incorporate into the students' academic experience the development of a lifelong learning process that promotes competency that serves the current job market and a good sense of citizenship. In this global economy, cultural awareness combined with the knowledge of a world language is a valuable asset to our students' education.

Reference

Shoemaker, Betty J.E. *Integrative Education: A Curriculum for the Twenty-First Century*. Oregon School Study Council, vol. 33, no. 2, 1989.

Teaching material references

Brasil, Brasil—A Tale of Four Cities. BBC, 2016, Dailymotion.
Brasil, Brasil—Samba to Bossa Nova. BBC, 2011, YouTube.
Brasil, Brasil—Tropicalia Revolution. BBC, 2013, YouTube.
Brazil Revealed. Directed by Graham Booth, Discovery Atlas, 2006.
Capoeira: The Dance of Freedom. 2013, YouTube.
Favela Rising. Directed by Jeff Zimbalist and Matt Mochary, Magnolia, 2010.
Gods of Brazil—Festour. 2013, YouTube.
Inside Rio Carnaval (2007). National Geographic, 2012, YouTube.
Kaapor Indians—Brazil Amazon. 2010, YouTube.
Lineker in Brazil: The Beautiful Game. BBC, 2016, YouTube.
Miracle Man: John of God. Discovery Channel, 2016, YouTube.
Page, Joseph A. *The Brazilians*. Perseus Book Group, 1995.
Waste Land. Directed by Lucy Walker, Arthouse Films, 2010.
Wide Angle—Brazil in Black and White. PBS, 2016.

14 Culture and language appreciation in a history of Latin America course

Beatriz García Glick

Course Title: Spanish 131: Ibero-American Civilizations
Course Level: Freshman or Sophomore
Language(s) in Focus: Spanish, Portuguese, Quiché or K'iche'
Course Type: Humanities, International Cultures

Contextualization of topic

Ibero-American Civilizations is a survey course of the history of Latin America from pre-Colombian to modern times. Because this course discusses the history of about 26 different countries from North, Central, and South America, students are exposed to many terms in various languages including Spanish, Portuguese, and Quiché which is one of the languages spoken by the Maya people. The course provides an opportunity for students to develop an appreciation for the subjectivity of translation since many words, concepts, and terms cannot be fully defined unless related to texts and a specific historical period. It is also a means to develop some grammar points which allow students to make comparisons between English and other languages. Finally, a study of the etymology of words gives students the confidence to approach the study of other languages.

Course logistics

Ibero-American Civilizations is a 3-credit-hour course that is taught online as a semester long course. It is a general core course required for graduating with various degrees in the Bachelor of Arts program. There are no prerequisites for this course, which is taught in English and includes various language-specific lessons.

Course objectives

The course objectives are to

- Provide a broad, general introduction to the lands, peoples, and history of Latin America
- Inform the student about the regions' ethnic diversity, cultural background, and problems of development
- Promote appreciation for the values and practices of other cultures, and a better understanding of relations between the nations of the regions and the United States

Learning outcomes

At the end of the course, the student should be able to

- Discuss general threads related to the development of most Latin American nations
- Explain in detail how various groups were affected first by the colonization and invasion of European nations, then by independence, and later by the world economic systems
- Compare and contrast the differences and similarities between the development of nations in Latin America with that of the United States
- Evaluate the advantages and disadvantages that most of Latin America faces with many European nations and the United States, based on economic theories including the Theory of Dependency
- Recognize and demonstrate the use of language and the difficulties in translation encountered by Spanish and Portuguese speakers in Latin America

Curricular structure

This online course is organized into 11 modules that follow the chapters of the main text, *Latin America: An American History*. In each module there are PowerPoint slides with speech recordings of each lecture. In order to gain a deeper understanding of Ibero-American Civilizations, there are various discussions on topics such as the historical, political, and linguistic factors embedded in the terms "Latin America" and "Civil Wars in Latin America as Destabilizing Factors." Some chapters have additional material presented to the students in the form of movies, like one pertaining

Culture and language appreciation 143

to the Maya Code, and readings such as the *Popol Vuh: The Sacred Book of the Maya*, where students are introduced to the language, culture, and sociological ideas of the Maya people by reading parts of the text and learning about the difficulties of translation from Quiché or K'iche' to English. Three lectures introduce the linguistic differences and similarities between Spanish and Portuguese. All of these lectures are based on the Spanish and Portuguese glossary at the end of the textbook.

The evaluation criteria are based on the following:

(50%) Five online exams of the textbook chapters and any ancillary material that pertains to each chapter
(10%) Online discussions
(40%) Semester-long project entitled "Historical Reflections" that entails the student's personal analysis of a specific nation's development from pre-Colombian to modern times

Theoretical framework

Because this is an online course, it follows the principles of the Universal Design for Learning Framework as proposed by Rose et al. who advocate that in order to make a course "accessible and appropriate for individuals with different backgrounds, learning styles, abilities, and disabilities...the course should stimulate the three major learning networks: Recognition, Strategic, and Affective by presenting flexible methods of presentation, expression, and engagement" (70–75). In order to individualize learning, it is not enough to use traditional fixed media based on text, image, and speech, but one must add flexible digital media which is versatile, transformable, editable, and interconnected. So, in this course, there are traditional lessons with interactive quizzes that assess one aspect of students' learning. To activate strategic networks, there are Discussion Forums where students interact and learn from each other utilizing strategies such as skimming, searching for context cues, logic, hypothesis testing, and other top-down processing as well as more deductive processing including the capacity to translate particular words in Spanish, Portuguese, and Quiché or K'iche'. Finally, to engage and address the affective networks of the students, there are student-driven projects such as the evolution of a particular group or class of people in a particular country throughout history, such as farmers in Mexico. These projects create versatile, transformable, editable, and interconnected examples of students' understanding of the material.

Teaching materials

Books

- *Latin America: An Interpretive History*, Julie Charlip and Bradford Burns, 2011
- *The Popol Vuh: The Sacred Book of the Maya*, Allen Christenson, (ed.), 2007
- *Black in Latin America*, Henry Gates, 2011

Films

- *Conquistadors*, David Wallace, 2001
- *Guns, Germs and Steel*, Jared Diamond, 2005
- *The Cracking of the Maya Code*, David Lebrun, 2008
- *Fidel Castro: The Untold Story*, Estela Bravo, 2001

Class activities

Since this is an online course, students are expected to read and to listen to the PowerPoint lessons, as well as to complete all online exercises after brief discussions on various topics within the course. The foreign language component is taught as additional online PowerPoint lessons with the following activities in order to give students a more complete understanding of the vocabulary in Spanish, Portuguese, and other languages which pertains to this course.

➢ Common Spanish Words in the English Dictionary
  Students were instructed to use the glossary of Spanish, Portuguese, and Indigenous terms in the textbook to identify words in Spanish that are or were part of the English vocabulary. For example, *contras, indio/india, Junta, maquiladora, mestizo/mestiza, mulato/mulata, negro/negra,* and *pueblo*. Then the following questions were posed:

- Do you know what they mean?
- Have you heard them or read them in articles?
- Can you give specific examples?

➢ Miscegenation in Latin America
  Students are asked to view the 18th-century oil painting entitled *Human Races* (*Las Castas*) which is kept in the Museo Nacional del Virreinato in Mexico and reproduced in the textbook. The purpose of the activity is to familiarize students with some of the nouns in Spanish and Portuguese that described racist practices

in Colonial Latin America. The painting depicts 16 different types of miscegenation, in four tiers where there are male/female pairs, each labeled according to racist practices in Colonial times. Regarding the painting, the following questions are posed:

- What do the following words mean in English? *lobo, mulato, gíbaro/jíbaro, zambo, mazombo*
- What are people compared to? (*Lobo* is a wolf, *mulato* refers to a mule, *gíbaro* is an Indian, *zambo* is a bow-legged person, and *mazombo* is a person born in Brazil whose parents were both European).

➢ Nouns in Spanish and Portuguese have Grammatical Gender
Students use the glossary of Spanish, Portuguese, and Indigenous terms from the textbook to learn about the grammatical gender of words in Spanish and Portuguese. In both languages, nouns have grammatically gendered meaning and all nouns are assigned a gender: masculine or feminine. For example, friend is *amigo/amiga* in both Spanish and Portuguese, and the "o" ending depicts masculine gender and the "a" expresses feminine gender. Table is *mesa* in both Spanish and Portuguese, so it is assigned the feminine gender because the word ends in the vowel "a."
Next, I invite students to determine the gender of nouns found in the glossary such as *adelantado, aldeia, arpillera, audiencia, cabildo, campesino, casa, ejido, fazenda, gaucho, hacienda, mazombo, mestizo, pueblo, quilombo, relaçao, senado,* and *sesmaria.*

➢ Possession in Spanish and Portuguese with the Preposition *de/do/da*, which means "of" in English
Once students are aware of the use of grammatical gender in Spanish and Portuguese, they also are given an explanation regarding one of the ways to indicate possession by means of the prepositions *de/do/da* all of which are translated to "of." In Spanish, in general, the preposition *de* suffices to join two nouns regardless of gender, but in Portuguese, there are two forms *do/da*. Since students understand grammatical gender, they can easily deduce that if a noun is masculine, the preposition "of" is *do* and if the noun is feminine, the preposition "of" is *da*. So, students are asked to view examples of this preposition in the glossary of Spanish, Portuguese, and Indigenous terms of the textbook including *Casa de Contratación* or Board of Trade, *Consejo de las Indias* or Council of the Indies, *Gente de pueblo* or Common people, and *Senado da Câmara* or Town Council.

➢ Notion of Duality or Parallelism in the *Popol Vuh*
The class travels virtually to the Guatemalan highlands in the year 1221, as they read parts of the *Popol Vuh* or *Book of the Community* (64). A literal translation of the book title is that *Pop* means "mat," like a woven mat used as a throne, and *vuh* refers to Maya codices or books painted on deerskin or bark paper. This book narrates the traditions, and mythical interpretations of various Mayan lineages of deities like "Striking Jaguar" or *Tukum B'alam*, and "Heart Sky" or *K'ux Kaj*.

Two of the main heroes of this book are the twin gods *Hunahpu* and *Xbalenque*. It is important to learn their pronunciation in K'iche' by using the modified Latin letters which Christenson explains in his book: "the h is pronounced like the English h but deeper in the throat. Similar to the Spanish j or the German ch as in Bach. The x is pronounced like the sh as in "shy" (55–56). To help students understand this pronunciation, the instructor spells their names *Hunahpu/Chunahpu* and *Xbalenque/SHbalenque*.

Since the notion of duality is present throughout the *Popol Vuh*, students are asked to read "The Descent of *Hunahpu* and *Xbalenque* into *Xibalba*/Underworld" to explain the duality of pairing in as many forms as they can find, including the following:

- Use of identical words
- Use of synonyms, such as Framer *Aj Tz'aq* and Shaper *Aj B'it*
- Use of antonyms, such as Day or *Q'ijil* and Night or *Aq'ab'al*
- Use of kinship
- Use of male/female gender association, such as "She Who Has Borne Children," corresponds with *Alom* and "He Who Has Begotten Sons" with *K'ajolom*

Ideas for future class activities

Although this course contains recorded files of the lectures, the students are not required to give oral presentations. This is something that needs to be addressed by adding recorded student presentations in the form of VoiceThreads, Podcasts, or recorded Blogs where the students could summarize or defend one of the ideas developed in the semester-long project. There could also be a dialogue with a person from a different time period who expresses their concerns about issues such as colonization, slavery, independence, the North Atlantic Free

Trade Agreement (NAFTA), neoliberalism, religious indoctrination, unjust laws, the segregation of women, civil war, or any other relevant theme. The speech would then be evaluated by peers who would add their points of view based on their interpretation of texts.

A voice recording would also encourage students to use foreign language vocabulary words.

Evaluation

The course assessments are based on two types of assessments. The formative assessments are the chapter exams, and the online discussions. The summative assessment is the reflective semester-long project that presents the student's analyses of various historical events that affected a country of their choice. This project is evaluated using the rubric below:

- (25%) Overall response to classmates' blogs
- (25%) Intellectual engagement with key concepts
- (25%) Personal response to key concepts
- (25%) Engaged writing

Although there are many Spanish, Portuguese, and K'iche' vocabulary terms that the students need to understand, any language elements are evaluated in bonus questions so that students who are not comfortable with languages will not feel that they are at a disadvantage.

Caveats and reflections

Span 131: Ibero-American Civilizations is a survey course that was not originally intended to teach any linguistic material. However, because of the extensive references to Spanish and Portuguese words to describe the legal, social, and political conditions that occurred more than 500 years ago, it is important to address language in context and to explain some grammatical notions that aid students in their comprehension of different worldviews and perspectives. One of the weaknesses of this course is the breadth of its scope. Students are exposed to historical events from pre-Colombian civilizations to NAFTA, and they are expected to understand general themes that affected more than 26 different countries. This is a lot for students to master.

The linguistic ideas such as grammatical gender and cosmic parallelism are woven into the course, but any assessment of language analysis is in the form of extra credit points on chapter quizzes, following the rationale that students did not sign up to learn another language in this course that is advertised as a course taught in English. The linguistic explanation of gender in Spanish and Portuguese is given to improve students' comprehension of the vocabulary that they need to study. The introduction to some K'iche' words also aims to enhance their appreciation of the difficulties in translation of words and terms from one culture to another and to expose students to cosmic interpretations that differ from their own realities. The hope is that this survey course will also stimulate students to research associations between words in other languages and to appreciate how much of the culture of the United States is based on that of other nations, in part through military and economic interventions by various countries, as well as through the migrations of people from several continents to and from Latin America.

Reference

Rose, David H., et al. *Teaching Every Student in the Digital Age: Universal Design for Learning.* Association for Supervision and Curriculum Development, 2002.

Teaching material references

Charlip, Julie A., and E. Bradford Burns. *Latin America: An Interpretive History.* 9th ed, Prentice Hall, 2011.
Christenson, Allen J., editor. *Popol Vuh: The Sacred Book of the Maya.* University of Oklahoma Press, 2007.
Conquistadors. Directed by David Wallace, PBS Home Video, 2001.
Cracking the Maya Code. Directed by David Lebrun, PBS Home Video, 2008.
Fidel Castro: The Untold Story. Directed by Estela Bravo, Bravo Films, 2001.
Gates, Henry L. Jr. *Black in Latin America.* New York University Press, 2011.
Guns, Germs, and Steel. Directed by Jared Diamond, PBS Home Video, 2005.

15 Heroes and Heroínas: teaching myths and legends through Hispanic culture

Tiffany Gagliardi Trotman

Course Titles: SPAN 250 Myths and Legends in Hispanic Culture
SPAN 350 Myths and Legends in Hispanic Culture
Course Level: Intermediate and Advanced
Language(s) in Focus: Spanish
Course Type Spanish Culture, General Humanities

Contextualization of topic

Within this course, students explore the function of myths and legends from a theoretical perspective while also reflecting on stories that form part of their own cultural identities. Creation myths, sacred spaces, gods and goddesses, heroes and tricksters, concepts of the afterlife, as well as 20th-century cultural myths, and the role of festivals serve as key themes through which students develop an enhanced appreciation of Hispanic culture.

Course logistics

This is a semester-long course consisting of 39 contact hours, with an expectation of an additional 141 hours consisting of noncontact, self-directed study, and assessment preparation. The class meets for three, 1-hour, discussion-based seminars per week. The course is multileveled and available to students at either the 200 or the 300 level. It is an option for both the Spanish major and minor as well as for students studying outside of the discipline, as no previous knowledge of Spanish language is required. The prerequisites for the 200-level and 300-level courses are the equivalent of two or three previous courses within the humanities, respectively.

Course objectives

The course objectives are as follows:

- Students will gain an understanding of the function of myths and legends within ancient and modern cultures with a particular focus on Hispanic culture.
- Students will read and analyze several theoretical approaches to understanding myths.
- Students will discuss and interpret key myths from both Latin American and Spanish cultures including myths of creation, destruction, and the afterlife, as well as stories of gods and goddesses. In addition, they will explore the importance of Pre-Colombian sacred sites.
- Students will identify legendary figures from Spanish culture, explore myths related to the unity of Spain, and discuss the importance of festival culture in Spain.
- Students will explore differences and similarities between the myths and legends that contribute to their own cultural identity and Hispanic myths and legends.
- Students will engage with a variety of cultural texts including written texts, painting, film, and ceramics to identify the manifestation of myths and legends within cultural artifacts, ancient and contemporary.
- Through active discussion and group work tasks, students will develop their communication and teamwork skills as they construct knowledge as a class.
- Students will engage with a variety of resources through research and present a cohesive written project on a specific relevant topic. They will synthesis this material into an engaging, short presentation.
- Advanced level students will develop enhanced communication skills as they facilitate a short class seminar on a specific topic within the course.

Learning outcomes

Upon successful completion of this course, students will be able to

- Demonstrate an understanding of fundamental concepts and principles of culture including the role of myths and legends in the development of cultural identity

Heroes and Heroínas 151

- Generate insights into social, cultural, and historical dimensions of cultural and subcultural groups within the Hispanic world
- Express self-awareness through critical reflections on the influence of myths and legends within their own culture
- Demonstrate an ability to acquire, organize, analyze, and evaluate information, taking into consideration the principles of academic integrity
- Demonstrate an ability to critically analyze a broad range of cultural phenomena through research, writing, and small-group discussion
- Effectively communicate research by oral presentation

In addition to the Learning Outcomes above, SPAN 350 students will also be able to

- Effectively facilitate seminar discussion

Curricular structure

This course was developed for both Spanish students and English-only students who have an interest in Hispanic Culture. To that end, the design required careful thinking about relevant content available in English and/or Spanish with an English translation. In addition, backward design was essential to the development of assessment tasks to ensure that students engaged with institutional graduate attributes.

Tables 15.1 and 15.2 below show the grading criteria for the SPAN 250 and SPAN 350 courses, respectively.

Table 15.1 Assessment Chart for SPAN 250 Course (Intermediate)

Type of Task	Percentage (%)
Essay Proposal	15
Essay	45
Tests (2)	$2 \times 10 = 20$
Research Presentation	15
Participation/Teamwork	5

Table 15.2 Assessment Chart for SPAN 350 Course (Advanced)

Type of Task	Percentage (%)
Essay	45
Research Presentation	10
Seminar Leadership	20
Test (2)	2 × 10 = 20
Participation/Teamwork	5

Detailed descriptions of assessment components are provided below.

- Essay Proposal (200-level only): 300-level students are also encouraged to write a proposal, however, it is not submitted for assessment. Students clarify and define a topic and write a provisional outline and timeline to guide the research process.
- Tests: There are two tests, each consisting of a series of short-answer questions.
- Participation/Teamwork: This course is discussion-based and knowledge and understanding will be developed through active participation and engagement with others in discussion-based activities. Students with Spanish proficiency should engage in discussion with others with a similar proficiency level.
- Essay: Topics require the approval of the course coordinator. The essay should be well investigated and use a variety of resources.
- Research Presentation: Students share the projects they have been working on during the semester.
- Seminar Leadership (300-level only): Seminar leadership includes the facilitation of discussion around an assigned topic. Students are expected to read beyond the topic and to develop a series of questions or subjects to engage classmates in discussion/debate around their understanding/interpretation/reflections. They may choose to bring related supplemental information such as images, videos, or music.

Theoretical framework

This course follows a thematic approach with each week of the course examining a distinct topic within the course. As with most course design, the introduction to the course moves from broad to more specific in the initial two weeks. Because Hispanic culture is extremely diverse, for the purpose of organization, the material has been divided into two halves with the first part of the course focused primarily on mythology from Latin America and the second half focused on Spanish

Table 15.3 Thematic Units

Week	Topic/Theme
1	Introduction
2	Understanding Myths and Legends
3	Myths of Creation
4	Sacred Spaces
5	Gods and Goddesses
6	The Afterlife and the End of the World
7	Film Screening
8	Legends from Spain: Invaders and Heroes
9	Trickster Myths • Don Juan • the Picaresque
10	Spanish Cultural Identity: The Myth of One Spain
11	Ferias and Festivales

legends and myths. Table 15.3 is a section from the course syllabus outlining the thematic units for each week of the semester.

Teaching materials

Representative books and films are listed here with other materials included in the References section.

Books

- *Intercultural Communication: A Contextual Approach*, James W. Neuliep, 2018
- *Mythology for Storytellers: Themes and Tales from around the World*, Howard J. Sherman, 2014
- *The Anthropology of Religion: An Introduction*, Fiona Bowie, 2006
- *Aztec and Maya Myths*, Karl Taube, 2012
- *The Trickster of Seville*, Tirso De Molina, 1963
- *Lazarillo de Tormes*, Anonymous, 1554

Film

- *Coco*, Lee Unkrich, 2017

Class activities

Classroom activities are organized using discussion-based teaching and learning. Students are predominantly responsible for creating the knowledge in class with the facilitator providing the framework or exercise that will scaffold this process. Each class typically uses a discussion activity developed by Stephen D. Brookfield and Stephen Preskill to facilitate an exploration of the assigned material. Specifics on these exercises can be found in *Discussion as a Way of Teaching: Tools and Techniques for University Teachers.*

Below is a selection of class activities that are specifically designed to foster discussion within the classroom in both Spanish and English. Students are typically grouped or paired with other students at a similar language level. Those without Spanish are grouped with beginning-level Spanish students for the purpose of discussion (Table 15.4).

> ➢ The Circle of Voices: Each person has an equal chance to contribute to the discussion, which sets up respectful boundaries for this discussion-based class.
> ➢ The Circle of Objects: Used to build cross-cultural understanding within a cohort, each student brings an object that reflects something about their culture or ancestry.
> ➢ Relaxed Buzz Groups: A student is given the role of "expert" and has the responsibility of sharing key information on the subject matter that should be supported by visual imagery to reinforce the concepts. Presentations may be done partly in English and Spanish.

Table 15.4 Weekly Class Activities

Week	Class Activities
1	Circle of Voices on "What Is Culture?" (Brookfield, pp. 63–64) Circle of Objects on "A myth that is important to me" (Brookfield, pp. 104–105)
2	Relaxed Buzz Groups on the readings (Brookfield, p. 82) Jigsaw "Important names in mythography" (Brookfield, pp. 87–88)
3	Drawing Discussion on the readings (Brookfield pp. 96–97)
4	Relaxed Buzz Groups on the documentaries (Brookfield, p. 82)
5	Drawing Discussion on the readings (Brookfield pp. 96–97)
6	Relaxed Buzz Groups on the death and the afterlife in your own culture (Brookfield, p. 82)
8	O'Roark, Ernest. "Will the Real El Cid Please Stand Up"
9	Drawing Discussion on *Lazarillo de Tormes* (Brookfield pp. 96–97)
10	Critical Debate (Brookfield pp. 89–90) Sentence Completion Exercise (Brookfield pp. 56–57)
11	Selection of short documentaries on specific Spanish festivals—Spanish with subtitles

➤ Drawing Discussion: In small groups, students depict myths pictorially. Students are able to work in groups designed to meet their language level. Students without any language experience are placed with introductory level students and are able to use both English and Spanish in their discussion. The use of visual imagery by drawing the myth supports the development of Spanish vocabulary associated with the story.
➤ Jigsaw: This discussion activity involves students developing expertise and sharing it with others. From a short list, students select a topic for independent research prior to class. During class, students who have the same topic first meet in a small group to explore their understanding of the topic. Once they have pooled their insights, new small groups are formed that include at least one representative for each of the original topics. Each student expert then leads a discussion of his or her particular topic. These small groups end when all members of the group fully understand the topics discussed.
➤ Critical Debate: Students are asked which side they would naturally argue based on personal beliefs and then they are assigned to the opposite debating team. Teams are also based on language level. Through newspaper articles in both Spanish and English, documentaries, or news stories, students prepare arguments that are presented at several language levels (beginner to advanced).
➤ *Lazarillo de Tormes* Lesson Plan: In preparation for class, students are provided with readings in both English and Spanish. Those with one or more years of Spanish are assigned the Spanish version specifically. Students with no previous knowledge of Spanish are asked to read a minimum of two pages and identify cognates that could facilitate their understanding of the Spanish text. Students are asked to identify key vocabulary/terminology from the readings prior to attending class. In class, students collaboratively develop a short list of important terms/functional vocabulary in Spanish, associated with the assigned reading.
  • (15 min.) Students form discussion groups and are provided a series of comprehension and analytical questions about the text in Spanish or English.
  • (15 min.) In the case of *Lazarillo de Tormes*, which is episodic, students engage in a Drawing Discussion.
  • (15 min.) Students present their illustrations orally in English/Spanish to the class.
  • (5 min.) Students have the opportunity to ask questions or synthesize information as a group.

Ideas for future class activities

Future activities might include the enacting of myths using Spanish and English language depending on students' level of languages. In addition, it would be valuable to have the students provide some personal reflections on the readings in either Spanish or English on a shared blog space. These reflections can serve as a spark for discussion questions in class.

Evaluation

The course includes both formative (Essay proposal – intermediate-level only, Tests, Participation/Teamwork) and summative assessments (Research Presentation Seminar Leadership – advanced-level only). The evaluation presented here is for the essay.

The essay may be written in Spanish or English. Students with a lower level of Spanish may choose to write only the introduction or conclusion of the essay in Spanish. If possible, students are asked to develop an interdisciplinary topic that lies within the scope of the course but also highlights another interest that they may have. Previous topics include the following:

- Origins and contemporary commercialization of the Day of the Dead
- The role of distance running in Tarahumara indigenous culture
- A comparison between Aztec and Maori creation stories

The grading rubric for the essay is composed of four parts, each with an assigned value. Below are descriptors for assigning a value to each criterion.

Focus

- High (30): The paper has a clear thesis statement. This main point clearly controls the entire paper, and the scope is manageable given the length of the paper and the nature of the assignment.
- Middle (24): The paper is not completely controlled by a central thesis statement. A central point is evident, but the entire essay is not consistent with that point. The paper contains occasional digressions or irrelevancies.
- Low (18): The main topic of the paper is too broad given the length of the paper, or the central point is simply not clear. The paper may be fragmented, with multiple points receiving equal attention.

Heroes and Heroínas 157

Development and support

- High (40): The paper's major ideas are clearly and logically developed. The paper reflects sound reasoning, and the information is accurate. Readers should respect, if not agree with, the paper's logic. Major ideas are clearly explained through concrete, specific details.
- Middle (32): The paper's major ideas are unevenly developed. Major ideas are well developed as a whole, but occasional problems in examples, explanations, or accuracy are likely to confuse readers or cause them to question the writer's logic.
- Low (24): The development of the major ideas is lacking and/or confusing. Readers would likely find significant flaws in logic, accuracy, or explanations. Major ideas are barely supported or merely repeated. Generalizations are used when more specific evidence is needed.

Organization

- High (20): The presentation order is clear and logical. Paragraphs and sentences follow a reasonable, coherent sequence. Readers should rarely, if ever, question the connection between one idea and another. Transitions and/or headings effectively signal the relationships among the larger parts of the paper.
- Middle (16): The paper has an order in which points are discussed, but the relationships are sometimes forced or unclear. The organizational scheme is recognizable, but some thoughts are difficult to follow. The writer has a sense of grouping ideas in paragraphs, but some transitions are awkward or unclear.
- Low (12): The paper is haphazardly or confusingly arranged. Readers will struggle in connecting ideas, sentences, or paragraphs.

Mechanics

- High (10): The paper conforms to accepted conventions of grammar, punctuation, spelling, and capitalization in a variety of sentence lengths and types.
- Middle (8): There are a few errors in grammar, punctuation, spelling, and capitalization.
- Low (6): Errors interfere with the credibility of the writer or with the meaning of the paper. There are grammar or punctuation errors even in simple sentences, and the meaning in a few sentences is not clear because of errors.

Caveats and reflections

The course facilitates well an interdisciplinary approach to learning through its ability to engage students whose primary discipline may lay outside of languages but for whom that discipline provides a unique window into the study of mythology. This has been apparent through the unique contributions of students from disciplines such as anthropology, psychology, archaeology, and others. Language learning could be improved through a dedicated discussion period for students at specific language levels each week and/or the inclusion of a language-based blog on the learning platform, Blackboard, in which students can write reflections in Spanish. The course contributes to the Language and Cultures Program's goal of diversifying our cohort by attracting nonlanguage students into our courses and the university's graduate attributes, Global Perspectives and Cultural Understanding.

Teaching material references

Anonymous. "Lazarillo de Tormes." *Nine Centuries of Spanish Literature*, edited by Seymour Resnick and Jeanne Pasmantier. Dover Publications Inc., 1963, pp. 12–60.

Bowie, Fiona. *The Anthropology of Religion: An Introduction*. Blackwell Publishing, 2006, pp. 267–300.

Brookfield, Stephen D., and Stephen Preskill. *Discussion as a Way of Teaching: Tools and Techniques for University Teachers*. The Society for Research into Higher Education and the Open University Press, 1999.

Coco. Directed by Lee Unkrich, Walt Disney Pictures and Pixar Animation Studios, 2017.

De Molina, Tirso. "The Trickster of Seville." *Nine Centuries of Spanish Literature*, edited by Seymour Resnick and Jeanne Pasmantier. Dover Publications Inc., 1963, pp. 254–263.

Fernández Kelly, Patricia. "Death in Mexican Folk Culture." *American Quarterly*, vol. 26, no. 5, December 1974, pp. 516–535.

"Lands of Gold." *Lost Kingdoms of South America Episode 3*, Martin Kemp, BBC, 2013.

Neuliep, James W. *Intercultural Communication: A Contextual Approach*. Sage, 2018, pp. 18, 93–96.

O'Roark, Ernest. "Will the Real El Cid Please Stand Up." www.islamicspain.tv/For-Teachers/12_Will%20the%20Real%20El%20Cid%20Please%20Stand%20Up.pdf. Accessed 7 Apr. 2019.

"People of the Clouds." *Lost Kingdoms of South America Episode 1*, Martin Kemp, BBC, 2013.

Read, Kay Almere, and Jason J. González. *Handbook of Mesoamerican Mythology.* ABC-CLIO, 2000. Selection of Gods and Goddesses, pp. 12–17, 81–115, 140–146, 150–155, 180–182, 184–194, 200–207, 212–215, 222–228.

Sherman, Howard J. *Mythology for Storytellers: Themes and Tales from around the World.* Taylor & Francis Group, 2014, pp. 1–16.

Taube, Karl. *Aztec and Maya Myths.* University of Texas Press, 2012, pp. 54–67.

Thury, Eva M., and Margaret Klopfle Devinney. "The Hero with a Thousand Faces." *Introduction to Mythology.* Oxford University Press, 2013, pp. 185–191.

Torrecilla, Jesús. "Spanish Identity: Nation, Myth, and History." *Studies in 20th & 21st Century Literature*, vol. 33, no. 2, 2009, pp. 204–226.

Conclusion

This volume offers innovative ways to incorporate foreign language content and concepts into humanities courses taught in English. Our objective is to promote foreign languages and attract new language learners to foreign language classrooms, in light of declines in enrollments in humanities courses nationwide, and foreign language courses in particular. The contributions to this collection display the adept joining of foreign languages with humanities content courses in the areas of literature, linguistics, and culture. The chapters contained in this volume demonstrate effective strategies for teaching foreign language content and reflect the diversity and creativity of foreign language faculty overall.

In teaching foreign language content, the importance of language fundamentals cannot be overlooked. The use of vocabulary and pronunciation of foreign language terminology to promote literary and cultural competencies is presented in chapters by Kalinoski, Nogueira, and Trotman. In addition to these foundational elements of language, there are subtleties and nuances of language practice that take into account social topics such as gender issues, as seen in chapters by Takagi, Ito, and Ueno. Language contact and cross-cultural communication are explored by Ananth and Jia through the lens of sociolinguistics and sociocultural studies. In addition to the diversity of language elements that the contributors to this volume provide, there is also great variety among the languages themselves. Not only does this volume present approaches to introducing language content from commonly taught languages such as French, German, Italian, and Spanish, but also brings to the fore less commonly taught languages such as Chinese, Portuguese, and Japanese. Moreover, Lyons, Huntington, and Glick incorporate in their chapters the use of indigenous languages to further underscore the diversity and adaptability of languages that can be introduced in classes taught in English.

In addition to traditional classroom settings where students are exposed to literature, linguistics, and cultural subjects, this volume shows examples of this engaging content in new teaching and learning platforms. For example, study abroad courses represent an alternative format for delivering foreign language content in a humanities course. As manifested in Negrelli's chapter, the goal of such courses is to enhance students' intercultural communication and adjustment skills prior to a short-term study abroad program.

Likewise, digital humanities has emerged as an innovative platform for the inclusion of foreign language content in humanities courses. Allowing for the intersection of digital technologies and humanities content, new pathways are opened to classroom teaching that incorporate foreign language content. This can clearly be seen through Ryu's chapter on flash fiction and "twitterature." This volume conveys imaginative uses of realia in the classroom that include the very latest cultural references, elicited from digital artifacts, to promote a bilingual approach to the humanities. Contemporary electronic media and language are also central to Tashiro's chapter that utilizes digital *manga* stories related to college life and cultural components such as food, technology, and fashion.

New platforms for language content in humanities courses also promote new pedagogies used to infuse foreign languages into humanities content courses. The Reacting to the Past (RTTP) pedagogical framework, with its emphasis on role-play of historical events based on authentic texts, provides another robust platform to infuse foreign language content into a humanities course curriculum. While Sugimori's course utilizes "a simplified version" of RTTP, it sparks several ideas to introduce foreign language in innovative ways. For example, in focusing on a particular era or societal structure such as feudalism in a given society, RTTP could be adapted to role play a day in the life of a commoner interacting with a feudal lord. Additional skits could illustrate the domestic life of a farmer and his family, or a stage performance of songs and dances from that time. All of these activities could involve language use at various levels of proficiency and are adaptable to any well-documented sociocultural moment in the history of a given place. Since RTTP is still a relatively new approach in the field of foreign language education, colleges and departments must provide incentives to faculty to pursue this possibility. Support in the form of dedicated time apart from classroom teaching, research, or service; internal and external grant opportunities; and travel funding to attend workshops and conferences to develop expertise in this area would be beneficial to this endeavor.

The sample lessons in this book are transferable between languages and are highly adaptable. An approach to incorporating language content that addresses the question of untranslated words, for example, is not dependent upon the language being used. Likewise, the source of the language content examples—social media, advertising, music, and the like—are transferable across languages. Moreover, this volume contains examples of classes offered from introductory to intermediate and advanced levels that could easily be fine-tuned to accommodate a different level of student attainment. The content of advanced courses could be simplified to meet the needs of students at the beginning of their university study and examples from lower-level courses could be applied to advanced courses by adjusting the task that is being asked of the students. Additionally, the adaptability of these courses may be extended to include online formats. Several activities could easily be adopted as part of a study abroad curriculum as well. In this way, this volume presents a tremendous resource for educators who see the value in incorporating foreign languages into their content courses.

Although the chapters in this volume are based on undergraduate college courses, the ideas contained within this volume can be adapted to suit audiences at the graduate level as well as at the middle and high school levels. This may be accomplished by selecting an appropriate content area (based on the level and local needs) and then incorporating elements of foreign language. For example, at the middle school level, virtually any class or enrichment activity could incorporate words or phrases from languages that reflect the student population and community surroundings. Similarly a business class at the graduate level, where learning is more specialized, could incorporate vocabulary, behaviors, and concepts from French, Japanese, or Latin American business cultures and communications, for example, as reflected in their languages. These can then be used as seeds to introduce content. The underlying idea is to plant a sapling of foreign languages in not only humanities, but also in other fields such as business, mass communications, and the field of science, technology, engineering, and mathematics (STEM).

The stimulating ideas presented in this volume motivate and encourage innovation in the classroom, but also require an investment of time and energy. Faculty confronted with the need to incorporate foreign languages in courses with humanities content may face a lack of time and resources. As an advocate for the humanities and social sciences, Chris Morett contends that humanities teaching can be reinvigorated "if faculty are provided with model syllabi and ideas for projects, and they get to see how seamlessly this can be done within the existing course design" (par. 10). The present volume addresses this concern with a collection of concrete examples of courses where the incorporation of language content and humanities courses is already taking place. It is for this reason that this resource is invaluable; it provides an important pedagogical resource to empower foreign language faculty to effect curricular changes and innovations in their classrooms. Such changes will promote the relationship between language and content, primarily to appeal to new language learners but also to encourage continuing students to stay invested in language study.

Reference

Morett, Chris. "What We Should Be Teaching in the Humanities and Social Sciences." *The Teaching Professor.* 3 December 2018, www.teachingprofessor.com/topics/teaching-strategies/course-specific/what-we-should-be-teaching-in-the-humanities-and-social-sciences/. Accessed 27 April 2019.

Index

Note: **Bold** page numbers refer to tables.

acculturation 80–81
active learning 89
advertising 8, 66–67, 73–74, 163
Africa 21, 34, 137
African fiction 35; *see also* African literature
African literature 8, 34–35
Akan 34, 38, 41
American Council on Teaching Foreign Languages (ACTFL) 4, 36
analytical thinking 26; *see also* critical thinking
anime 45, 90, 92, 101–102, 107–108, 115–116
anthropology 134, 139, 158
approaches 3–6, 87, 150, 161
archaeology 158
Asian studies 43, 87, 104
assessment 7, 40, 65, 73, 88, 92, 147, 149, 151–152

backward design 26, 36, 44, 65, 88, 97, 126, 151
Baoulé 34, 38
base culture 124
behavioral culture 9, 124, 126
bilingual 8, 26, 38, 56; bilingual approach 8, 25, 32, 162; bilingualism 98
blog 146–147, 156, 158
Brazil 74, 133–137, 139–140, 145
business 34, **82**, 128, 163

capoeira 9, 133, 135, 137
carnival 9, 133, 135
cell phone novels 8, 25, 27
China 47, 97, 124, 129
Chinese 7–8, 48, 90, 96, 101, 118–119, 124–131, 161
Chinese behavioral culture 9, 124
cinematic works 34, 38; *see also* films
cognates 55, 155
collaborative learning 89
comics 116, 119
Common European Framework of Reference for Languages (CEFR) 36
commonly taught languages 161
communication 9, 22–23, 26, 32, 35, 41, 57, 77–80, 83–85, 100, 103, 105, 125, 131, 150
communication gaps 3
communities 3, 41, 74
comparative analysis 30; comparative linguistics 37
Content-Based Instruction (CBI) 5
conversation theory 18–19
cool Japan 9, 115
critical languages 1
critical thinking 4, 19, 22–23, 46, 49–50, 53, 64, 75, 89, 110, 125, 134
cross-cultural communication 9, 124–127, 129–130, 161; cross-cultural competency 43; cross-cultural understanding 50, 154; *see also* communication

Index

cultural artifacts 150; cultural awareness 19, 81, 134, 139–140; cultural competency 105; cultural hybridity 47; cultural identity 9–10, 149, 150, **153** (*see also* identity); cultural intelligence 4; cultural literacy 8; cultural norms 104
culture 3–4, 7–10, 16, 25, 31, 34–35, 49, 52, 57, 66, 77–84, 87–88, 90, 96, 104, 109–111, 115, 117, 120, 122, 124–128, **130**, 131, 133–134, 136, 139, 141–143, 148–151, 154, 156, 158, 161, 163
culture studies 104, 133

dialects 39
digital humanities 56, 162; digital media 143; digital portfolio 26; *see also* e-portfolio
digital technologies 25, 32, 162
disciplines 3–6, 9, 35, 134–137, 139, 158
discussion-based 17–18, 105–106, 139, 149, 152–154
diversity 4, 16, 34–35, 78, 93, 115, 117, 123, 125, 139, 142, 161
dual-language assignments 41

East Asian languages 103, 116; East Asian studies 96–97
electronic media 162
emoji 119–120, 122
enrollments 1, 2, 3–4, 6, 10, 161
e-portfolio 138
etymology 141
experiential learning 126
export model 5–6

"face" culture 125, 130
face-to-face 43, 64, 78, 97
family 23, 26, 39–40, 45, 90, 162
fashion 116–117, 162
film 8, 18, 22, 37, 40, 43–49, 52–55, 78, 83, 99, 101, 110, 117, 124, 144, 150, 153
flash fiction 8, 25–26, 28–32, 162
flipped classroom 78, 84
folktales 39
food 9, 66, 72–73, 116–117, 162
foreign language education 4–5, 9, 124, 162; *see also* foreign languages

foreign languages 1, 3–9, 20, 22, 50, 63–64, 66, 75, 103, 125–126, 161–163
Foreign Languages across the Curriculum (FLAC) 5–6
formative assessment 22, 49, 73–74, 83, 101, 129, 147; *see also* assessment
French 7–8, 15, 21–22, 34, 36–39, 98, 161, 163
futebol 133

game pedagogy 98
gender 9–10, 23, 34, 44, 46, 48, 73, 87, 89–91, 96, 104, 106–108, 145–148, 161; gender differences 9, 88, 97–98, 101; gender identities 104; gender roles 23, 45, 116–117; gender studies 104 (*see also* Women's and Gender studies); gendered language 87, 92
general education 8, 15, 35, 43, 52, 57, 88, 116
genre 8, 25–28, 30, 32, 53, 64, 117, 121
German 7–8, 15, 21–22, 146, 161
girl-graphs 9, 109
global competency 44; *see also* competency
global literature 8 (*see also* literature); global 3, 16, 25–26, 32, 35, 37, 41, 43, 58, 77–79, 85, 88, 105, 111, 131, 140, 158; global studies 43; globalization 64, 87, 117
Golden Age Literature 8, 52
grammar 3, 9, 26, 49, 84, 93, 96, 98, 101, 110, 128, **130**, 141, 157

heritage speakers 34, 37, 41
higher education 1, 23
hiragana 30, 49, 64, 96, 108–109, 118
Hispanic culture 10, 149–152
history 9–10, 38, 47, 58, 63, 66, 74, 89, 93, 96, 98, 116–119, 124, 134, 137, 139, 141–144, 162
honorifics 9, 87, 106; *see also* register
humanities 1, 3–10, 15–16, 25, 32, 52–54, 63–64, 75, 84, 116, 124, 133, 141, 149, 161–164
Humanities Departmental Surveys 3

identities 36, 41, 91, 104; *see also* identity
identity 8–9, 35, 37, 39, 104, 107, 109–110, 131
idol culture 45
import model 6
indigenous languages 161
inquiry-based 54, 105, 106
integrative/reflective thinking 16
intensive courses 117
intercultural communication 77, 85, 153, 162; *see also* communication
interdisciplinary 9, 75, 124, 133–134, 156, 158
international students 100, 102, 129
internship 140
Italian 8, 15, 22, 74, 161

Japan 9, 28, 45–47, 63–64, 66, 72–74, 77, 79–82, 88–89, 96, 99, 101, 103–104, 106–108, 110, 115, 118–119
Japanese animation 118 (*see also* anime); Japanese culture 25, 30, 43, 77, 79–80, 105, 115–116, 118, 122; Japanese English 49, 64, 66; Japanese literature 8, 43–44; Japanese Studies 25, 43
jigsaw 91, **154**, 155
J-pop 8, 66, 92

K'iche' 141, 143, 146–148; *see also* Quiché
kana 47, 109; *see also hiragana; katakana*
kanji 47–48, 96, 100, 108–110, 118–119
katakana 9, 47–49, 64, 71, 92, 96, 108–109, 115–118, 121–122
Korea 77, 81, 110; *see also* South Korea
Korean 77, 79, 81, 83, 92; *see also* Korea
K-pop 92

language contact 63–67, 73–74, 161; language learning 3, 5, 8, 10, 41, 75, 79–80, 84, 93, 97, 122, 126, 134, 158
language policies 8, 34
language proficiency 5–6, 37, 131; *see also* proficiencies; proficiency

Languages across the Curriculum (LAC) 5
Latin America 9–10, 141–142, 144–145, 148, 150, 163
legend 10, 53, 149–151, 153
less commonly taught languages 161
LGBTQ 45, 91–92, 110
linguistic analysis 28, 31; linguistics 7–8, 63–64, 75, 89, 96–97, 99, 104–105, 161–162; linguistics studies 64, 87
listening comprehension 136–138
literary analysis 16–17, 38, 50; literary criticism 17
literature 3, 7–8, 15–19, 23, 25, 34, 43, 44–46, 49–50, 53, 66, 93, 102, 116, 124, 161–162
loan words 9, 47

manga 45, 91, 115–117, 119–122, 162
marriage 45
mass communication 163
Maya 141, 143–144, 146
media 45–46, 49, 88, 91–93, 97, 110, 143
Meiji Period 43, 45, 96
metalanguage 18–19
methods 3–4, 58, 143
mimetic words 119
mnemonics 118
Modern Language Association (MLA) 1–3, 35
monolingual 38, 99
multiliteracies 8, 34–35, 37, 41
multimedia 17, 39, 41; multimedia technologies 41; *see also* digital technologies
myth 10, 99, 146, 149–151, 153, **154**, 155–156

narrative theory 53–54
National Endowment for the Humanities (NEH) 6
national language policies 34; *see also* language policies
nihonjinron 87
novels 8, 25, 52

online 10, 27–28, 74, 78, 83, 91, 98, 101, 116, 129, 141–144, 147, 163
onomatopoeia 115–116, 118–119, 121–122

oral communication 44, 88; oral literary traditions 39
orthographic 9, 96; see also orthography
orthography 71, 74, 101

pedagogy 5, 34, 58, 87, 98–99, 127
peer assessment 17; see also assessment
performance studies 124
pitch accents 101
plays 52
plurilingual 34, 37–39, 41; see also bilingual
podcast 29–30, 146
poetry 26, 52, 55
politeness 96–97, 106, 109
political science 134, 139
popular culture 9, 115–117, 133–134, 139–140; popular music 133, 135, 137
Portuguese 7–9, 133–145, 147–148, 161
power 9, 21, 29, 38, 48, 53, 93, 104, 108
Pre-Colombian 141, 143, 147, 150
print media 8, 66; see also media
problem-solving skills 32
proficiency 5–6, 25, 32, 36–37, 41, 102–103, 131, 152, 161; proficiencies 32, 37
project-based 27, 36, 89
pronoun 88–91, 98, 101, 107–109
pronunciation 47–48, 56, 58, 98, 100, 128, 136–138, 146, 161
proverbs 39
psychology 5, 158

Quiché 141, 143

race 10, 144
Reacting to the Past (RTTP) 9, 96, 98–99, 100–103, 162
reading comprehension 16, 22, 30
realia 162
recruit 129; recruiting 5, 50; recruitment 74
reference terms 89–91; see also pronouns

reflective thinking 16
regional dialects 9, 88; see also dialects
register 21, 39, 87
religion 116–117, 134, 136–137, 153
retention 20, 50, 74
ritual expressions 128–129
role-play 98–99, 101–102, 124, 162
romanization 71–72
rubrics 54, 83

second language acquisition 66
self-assessment 17; see also assessment
semiotic processes 98
service-based learning 140; see also service-learning
service-learning 80–81, 83
sexist language 9, 108; sexuality 104
short-term study abroad (SA) 9, 77–81, 83, 84, 162; see also study abroad
social media 163
sociocultural 5, 9, 77, 79, 81, **82**, 83–85, 87–89, 92, 161;
sociolinguistics 9, 63, 77, 96, 99, 102–105, 109–110, 161; sociology 134
songs 17, 39, 84, 162
South Korea 110
Spain 52–53, 58, 150, **153**
Spanish 7–8, 10, 15, 20, 22, 52–58, 74, 141–152, **153**, 154–156, 158, 161
speaking 43–44, 100, 138
speech styles 87
STEM 4, 163
stereotypes 21, 46, 88, 97; stereotypical 106–107, 115
student-centered 84, 105
study abroad 73, 74, 124, 139, 162–163
subtitling 22
summative assessment 7, 22, 49, 56, 74, 83, 101, 110, 122, 125, 130, 147, 156; see also assessment

target culture 124, 127; target language 5–6, 8, 126
task-based 27

technology 9, 83, 116–117, 119, 162–163
thematic 17, 26, 29, 35–36, 40, 66, 79, 98, 117, 152–153; thematic approach 152 (*see also* approach); theme-based 45, 66, 135
transcultural competence 3; *see also* competence
translation 8, 15–16, 19, 21, 25–32, 34, 37–39, 43, 46, 48, 50, 56, 91, 97, 102–103, 108, 128, 141–143, 146, 148, 151
translingual 3, 8, 34, 36–41; transnational 3
trendy words 49
twitterature 8, 25, 27–29, 162

universal design 143

vocabulary 9, 73, 84, 93, 117–118, 121, 134, 137–138, 144, 147–148, 155, 161, 163

web material 56
Wolof 21
women 8, 43–46, 49, 89, 91, 93, 101, 104, 106–108, 147
Women's and Gender studies 43; *see also* Women's studies
women's language 87–89
Women's studies 104; *see also* Women's and Gender studies
world language 140; world literatures 15
World Readiness Standards for Learning Languages 35
writing 25–26, 36–38, 40, 44, 46–47, 57, 64, 72, 81, 93, 104, 109, 117–118, 134, 136–139, 147, 151
writing system 9, 47, 66, 84, 88–89, 96, 98, 108, 115, 118–119; *see also* orthography

Yoruba 34, 39, 41

For Product Safety Concerns and Information please contact our EU representative GPSR@taylorandfrancis.com
Taylor & Francis Verlag GmbH, Kaufingerstraße 24, 80331 München, Germany

www.ingramcontent.com/pod-product-compliance
Lightning Source LLC
Chambersburg PA
CBHW051646230426
43669CB00013B/2455